The complete works of Percy Bysshe Shelley ... Volume 1

Shelley, Percy Bysshe, 1792-1822, Dole, Nathan Haskell, 1852-1935

Queen Mab

The Dæmon of the World

Alastor

The Complete Works of
PERCY BYSSHE SHELLEY

—✦✳✦—

QUEEN MAB

AND OTHER POEMS

EDITED BY

Nathan Haskell Dole

Illustrated

London and Boston
Virtue & Company
Publishers

Contents

List of Illustrations

———•———

Introduction

———◆———

ALTHOUGH Shelley wrote narrative poems and one great tragedy, his genius was primarily lyrical, and his poetry tells more to a reader who is acquainted with his character and the events of his life than to one who knows the poems only as if they had fallen out of the air from some invisible singer. No poet ever sang more directly out of his own feelings — his joys, his sorrows, his desires, his regrets; and what he has written acquires a fuller meaning when we understand its source and its occasion. Shelley's poetry belongs also to a particular epoch in the world's history — the revolutionary epoch — and what may fairly be described as the body of doctrine

Introduction

which forms the intellectual background of his imaginative visions can be comprehended only when we consider his work in relation to the period of which it is the outcome. "A beautiful and ineffectual angel, beating in the void his luminous wings in vain"—so Matthew Arnold, with a variation of Joubert's sentence on Plato,[1] defined his conception of Shelley. The charm of the phrase must not render us insensible of its remoteness from the fact. Shelley was no angel, whether of celestial or diabolic race, but most human in his passions, his errors, his failures, his achievement. Nor was it in the void that he lived and moved; he belonged in an eminent degree to the revolutionary movement of his own day, and viewed apart from the teaching of that geometer of the Revolution whom he accepted as his master—William Godwin—the work of Shelley is only half intelligible.

Percy Bysshe Shelley was born on 4th August, 1792, at Field Place, near Horsham, Sussex. The family was ancient and honourable, but no ancestor of the poet had ever given

[1] "Plato loses himself in the void, but one sees the play of his wings, one hears their rustle," quoted by Matthew Arnold in his essay on Joubert.

proof of literary genius. His grandfather, Bysshe Shelley, who received a baronetcy in 1806, had accumulated a large fortune, had married two heiresses, had quarrelled with his children, and now, troubled with gout and the infirmities of age, lived somewhat penuriously in a cottage house at Horsham. Timothy Shelley, the poet's father, was a country gentleman — dull, consequential, irritable, but not unkindly in disposition, who in the House of Commons gave an unwavering vote for the Whig party, and who was secured from all risk of aberration from the social conventions by a happy inaccessibility to ideas. His wife, Elizabeth, daughter of Charles Pilfold, of Effingham, Surrey, was beautiful in person, and a woman of good sense, when her good sense was not obscured by temper. Though no lover of literature, she was an excellent letter-writer.

Percy, the eldest child, inherited his mother's beauty. He was slight of figure, of fair and ruddy complexion, with luminous blue eyes, and hair curling naturally, which changed from golden to a rich brown; in temperament gentle yet excitable, of rare sensibility, prone

Introduction

to yield up his imagination to fantastic tale or vision, but not devoid of a certain quaint mirthfulness which took delight in oddity and surprises. Having acquired some knowledge of Latin from a neighbouring country parson, he was sent at ten years old to Sion House Academy, Isleworth, where Doctor Greenlaw taught some fifty or sixty boys, chiefly of the social middle class, and where Shelley's cousin, Thomas Medwin, was a pupil. The rough tyranny of the elder lads, who looked on the new scholar as strange and unsocial because he was sensitive and shy, sometimes drove him to violent outbreaks of passion; yet, says his schoolfellow Rennie, "if treated with kindness, he was very amiable, noble, high-spirited, and generous." Here Shelley made some progress in classical learning; his sense of intellectual wonder was much stimulated by scientific lectures; and his heart awoke to the new and exquisite pleasure of romantic attachment to a boy of about his own age, whom he describes as of a character eminently generous, brave, and gentle.

In 1804 he passed from Sion House Academy to Eton, at that date under the head-

Introduction

mastership of Doctor Goodall, an excellent scholar and kindly gentleman, but one who held the reins of authority perhaps somewhat too loosely. Shelley's tutor, George Bethell, with whom he boarded, was unluckily the dullest man in Eton; he had the merit, however, of being good-humoured and well-meaning. At Eton as at Sion House, Shelley stood apart from the throng of his schoolfellows. His spirit rose in rebellion against the system of fagging; he did not join in the school sports; he pursued studies in which his young coevals did not care to follow him. All things seemed to point out " mad Shelley" as a fit and proper victim upon whom the other boys might let loose their animal spirits. " I have seen him," wrote a schoolfellow, " surrounded, hooted, baited like a maddened bull." If it was his tormentors' wish to excite their victim to paroxysms of rage, they often attained the desired end. Yet here, as at his earlier school, he won the good-will of a few of his schoolfellows, who describe him as generous and openhearted, of remarkable tenderness of heart, possessed of much moral courage, and fearing nothing but what was false or low. No friend pleased him better than old Doctor Lind, of Windsor, a man original in character and opinions, and of most amiable temper. Shelley has given idealized portraits of this friend of his boyhood in Zonoras of " Prince Athanase " and the aged hermit of " The Revolt of Islam."

Shelley's interest in what we may term the romantic side of modern science increased during the Eton years. He read the classics with a delight in the beauty of the poetry and a keen interest in the philosophical views of certain writers, — among these Lucretius and Pliny, — but without showing much capacity for minute exactness of scholarship. The chief masters of his intellect were those eighteenth century thinkers who seemed to bring into a certain harmony the destructive or skeptical criticism of the age and those boundless hopes for the future which sprung phantomlike from the ruins of the past. He was too young to have learned the lessons of experience derived from the facts of the French Revolution, as they developed themselves from day to day. He accepted the doctrine of the *Aufklärung* from Godwin's " Political Justice " with awed

and delighted mind. With Condorcet he beheld as in a vision the endless progress of the
human race. His dreams were bright and generous dreams of youth, and in truth they were
not altogether of a baseless fabric. Much that
has become actual in the nineteenth century
has grown out of the visions and aspirations
of the age of revolution; much perhaps remains to be realized.

Two moments of boyhood memorable in
the development of his spirit have found
record in Shelley's verse, — that in which, escaping from the feelings of resentment and
revenge excited by the persecutions and tyran-
nies of school, he vowed, for his own part, to
be just, gentle, wise, and free; and that other
moment when his imagination, escaping from
the excitements of gross, fantastic horror, devoted its powers to the pursuit of spiritual
beauty. The record of one of these moments
will be found in the dedication of "The Revolt of Islam"; the record of the other in the
"Hymn to Intellectual Beauty." Both of
these inspirations of high resolve came in the
springtime, when the awakened life of nature
seemed to reinforce the vitality of the spirit.

Introduction

Before leaving Eton Shelley was an author. The romance of "Zastrozzi," published in April, 1810, was written, at least in great part, a year earlier. This and a second romance, "St. Irvyne, or the Rosicrucian," which appeared before the close of the same year, are indescribably but not unaccountably absurd in their crude efforts at sublimity, their overwrought horrors, their pseudo-passion, their sentimental inanities. The author, still a boy, was yielding an untrained imagination to the romantic movement of his day, as represented by its worst models, just as he had yielded his intellect in bondage, which fancied itself liberty, to the revolutionary speculators and dreamers. Shelley's boyish romances cease to be inexplicably bad when we have made acquaintance with certain Minerva Press novels of the same date; we see that he was only a disciple, not a creator, of the fantastic-absurd, to which Mrs. Radcliffe and M. G. Lewis had given a vogue, and which just at this date was satirized in "Northanger Abbey," the earliest novel of our most exquisite humourist of domestic life. A poem in several cantos on the subject of "The Wandering Jew" was

Introduction

written (1810) by Medwin and Shelley in conjunction; four cantos appeared after Shelley's death, but it is uncertain whether they contain more than a few lines from his hand. A thin volume of verse, entitled " Original Poetry by Victor and Cazire," the work of Shelley and another, actually saw the light in September, 1810; it was speedily withdrawn from circulation by the publisher on discovering the fact that one of the pieces was a transcript from the pages of M. G. Lewis. No copy of the " Original Poetry " is known to exist, and we can hardly regret the disappearance of verses which a reviewer describes, in all probability not unjustly, as " downright scribble."

It has been suggested that Shelley's coadjutor, who assumed the feminine name " Cazire," was his cousin Harriet Grove, a beautiful girl of his own age, whom he loved with a boy's first ardour, and whom he would fain have made a partner in his own social, political, and religious beliefs and disbeliefs. The tone of his correspondence alarmed Harriet's family, and before long they had another settlement for her in view. Shelley suffered, or imagined that he suffered, much, declaimed

Introduction

against bigotry, and was resolved henceforth
to wage bitter war against that destroyer of
human happiness.

Having matriculated at University College,
Oxford, in April, 1810, Shelley entered on
residence in Michaelmas term of the same
year. In his fellow student, Thomas Jeffer-
son Hogg, son of a north-country gentleman
of Tory politics, he found his closest ally.
Hogg had high intellectual powers and a genuine love of literature; his type of mind and
character was as remote from Shelley's as can
well be conceived; he was keen-sighted, shrewd,
sarcastic, but not devoid of some of the generosity of youth; and he was highly interested
in observing such a singular and charming phe-
nomenon among young Oxonians of the days
of the Regency as the idealist Shelley. Every
one who knows anything of Shelley's life
knows Hogg's admirable portrayal of Shelley at Oxford: every one has been an intimate with Hogg in the college chambers,
wildly confused with electrical and chemical
apparatus; has heard the eager discourse of
the young enthusiast concerning the mysteries
of nature and the deeper mysteries of mind;

xiv

has seen him at his favourite sports of skimming stones and sailing paper boats on river or pond; has strode across country with the pair in their joyous winter walks, and shared the frugal supper which they enjoyed on their return; has witnessed "the divine poet's" sweet humanity toward those who needed the sustenance of hand or heart, and no less his sudden outbreaks of indignation against the wrongdoer and the oppressor; has smiled with the narrator at the quaint freaks and fancies of the immortal child.

"The devotion, the reverence, the religion with which he was kindled toward all the masters of intellect," says Hogg, "cannot be described." The biographer speaks of the purity and "sanctity" of Shelley's life, of his "meek seriousness" of heart and "marvellous gentleness" of disposition. But with reverence for the self-elected masters of his intellect, and this marvellous gentleness, Shelly united a contempt for inheritance and tradition, and an intellectual audacity which was unchecked by any adequate sense of the difficulties encompassing the great problems of human thought. His guides were the lights of the eighteenth

Introduction

century illumination. Had he mastered Kant as well as Holbach, and submitted his intellect to Burke as he submitted it to Godwin, he might not have shot up as quickly, but his roots would have plunged deeper and embraced the soil more firmly. Yet it is hard to conceive Shelley as other than he actually was. And it may be that the logical gymnastic of his studies in eighteenth century thinkers — and those especially of France — saved him in some degree from the dangers of an excessive tendency toward the visionary. "Had it not been for this sharp brushing away of intellectual cobwebs," writes Mr. Salt, "his genius, always prone to mysticism and metaphysical subtleties, might have lost itself . . . in a labyrinth of dreams and phantasies, and thus have wasted its store of moral enthusiasm." Only we must remember that in the eighteenth century crusade against thrones and churches there was a good deal of visionary destructiveness, as events have proved, and that a part of Shelley's moral enthusiasm, as some of us venture to think, was not wisely directed.

Shelley's career at University College was

Introduction

brief. In February, 1811, a small pamphlet
entitled "The Necessity of Atheism" was issued
from a provincial press at Worthing in Sussex.
The author's name was not given, but in Oxford, where the pamphlet was offered for sale,
it was known to be the work of Shelley. On
being interrogated by the master of his college,
Shelley refused to answer the questions put to
him. The same questions were put to Hogg,
who had come forward to remonstrate with the
authorities; he also declined to reply, and on
25th March both youths were expelled from
University College for contumacy in refusing
to answer questions and declining to disavow
the publication.

"I *once* was an enthusiastic Deist," Shelley
wrote a few weeks later, "but never a Christian." His atheism was the denial of a creator
rather than the denial of a living spirit of the
universe. A Christian he never became in the
theological sense of that word; but certainly,
at a later time, he deeply reverenced the personal character of Jesus. And his militant
ardour against the historical developments of
Christianity in some degree waned as he became better acquainted with the literature and

art of mediæval Italy. His faith in later years had in it something of Plato's and of Berkeley's idealism; something perhaps also of the philosophic system of Spinoza.

A word must be said of the " Posthumus Fragments of Margaret Nicholson," which appeared in Shelley's first term at University College. Poems written with a serious intention, but bearing all the marks of immaturity, were put forth under cover of a jest, and were perhaps retouched — Hogg assisting — with a view to burlesque effect. Margaret Nicholson, a mad washerwoman, had attempted the king's life, and was now in Bedlam. It was decided that she should be the authoress of the verses, and that their publication should be posthumous, under the editorial supervision of an imaginary nephew, John Fitz-Victor. The pamphlet was brought out in quarto form; the mystification perhaps delighted the author, but we do not find it difficult to credit the publisher's statement that the work was almost still-born.

On quitting Oxford the two college friends resided for awhile together in London lodgings. Mr. Timothy Shelley refused to receive

Introduction

his son at Field Place unless he would undertake to break off all communication with Hogg, and submit himself to appointed tutors and governors. Such conditions Shelley declined to accept, and so remained in exile from his home with a sore feeling that he was unjustly punished for intellectual beliefs for which he was not morally responsible. On Hogg's departure to his friends, Shelley remained in lodgings alone. His younger sisters were schoolgirls at Clapham, and through them he had already made the acquaintance of their companion, Harriet Westbrook, a pink and white schoolgirl beauty of sixteen, with a pleasant temper, a bright smile, and a pretty manner, — the daughter of a retired London coffee-house keeper. Her guide and guardian, the elder Miss Westbrook, already thirty years old, showed a most affectionate interest in the young misbeliever, who was also a prospective baronet with a great property entailed, wrote to him, called on him with Harriet, conducted him to church, read under his guidance the works of heretics. When in the summer Shelley visited his cousin Mr. Grove at Cwm Elan in Radnorshire, the Westbrooks were also in

Introduction

Wales, and communications went to and fro between Shelley and the sisters. On the return of the Westbrooks to London urgent letters came from Harriet; she was persecuted in her home; they were about to force her to return to school, where she was miserable; should she resist her father, or would it be wrong to put an end to her life? Another letter came, in which she threw herself on Shelley's protection; she would fly with him if he were but willing. Shelley hastened to London, yet before he left Wales he found time to write to his cousin Charles, telling him that if he devoted himself to Harriet it was not for love's sake, but through a chivalrous motive of self-sacrifice. On seeing Harriet, he was shocked by her altered looks, which he ascribed to the suffering caused by domestic persecution; she now avowed that it was not so, that she loved him, and feared that he could not return her love. They parted with a promise on Shelley's part that if she summoned him from the country he would come quickly and unite his fate with hers. Within a week the summons arrived. Immediately arrangements for flight by the northern mailcoach were made, and on the 28th of August, 1811, Shelley and Harriet Westbrook, aged respectively nineteen and sixteen, joined hands as man and wife at Edinburgh, with such ceremony as the Scottish law required. It needed some straining of the principles of a disciple of William Godwin to submit to a legal form of marriage; but for the sake of Harriet's appearance in the eyes of the world he consented to what he regarded as an evil. He assured her that for his own part he did not consider the contract binding, if at some future time their union should prove a source of misery instead of happiness.' And in so far he was obedient to the teaching of his philosophic master.

In fact, at this time, Shelley was immeasurably more interested in a Sussex schoolmistress, Miss Hitchener, whom he had idealized into an Egeria or a Cythna, than in Harriet Westbrook. This very commonplace person became for his boyish imagination a type of all that is most exalted in womanhood, but his feeling was one of homage and rapture, not

' See Southey's last letter to Shelley in "Southey's Correspondence with Caroline Bowles"

a feeling of love, which could descend to the commonplace of wedlock. "Blame me if thou wilt, dearest friend," he wrote to her, when apologizing for his marriage, "for *still* thou art dearest to me; yet pity even this error if thou blamest me." A closer acquaintance with Miss Hitchener, a year later, resulted — after a fashion too common with Shelley — in an idealization of an opposite kind; the worthy woman assumed the form of a demon of self-ishness and ignoble passion, an angel indeed still, but of the diabolic kind.

Shelley's father had allowed him two hundred pounds a year before his marriage; now he saw fit to give the rash boy a lesson by cutting off supplies. Ultimately the allowance was again given, and with two hundred pounds also from Mr. Westbrook, the young couple were not in danger of want.

From Edinburgh they journeyed to York, where they passed under the control of the evil providence of their wedded life, the elder sister, Eliza Westbrook; and where misconduct of Hogg's caused a temporary breach between him and Shelley. From York they passed to Keswick, attracted in part by the

Introduction

fact that there resided Southey, for whose poetry Shelley at the time had a strong admiration. Southey received the young people with characteristic kindness, but to Shelley he seemed a spent force, a withered branch, because he took little interest in metaphysical subtleties, and had lost his early confidence in the virtue of revolutionary abstractions. A more congenial personal influence was that of William Godwin, with whom Shelley entered into correspondence while at Keswick; he laid bare his spirit before Godwin as before a philosophic confessor, listened to his direction with reverence, and hoped for the joy of a closer intimacy with this latest and greatest of the sages.

With his desire at once to translate his ideas into action for the service of the world, Shelley looked abroad for a battle-field where he might combat on behalf of freedom, and he found it, as he supposed, in Ireland. He prepared an Address to the Irish people, consisting, as he states it, "of the benevolent and tolerant deductions of philosophy reduced into the simplest language." He would plead on behalf of Catholic Emancipation, on behalf of the Repeal of the Union, he would endeavour to establish a system of societies in Ireland for the discussion of social, political, and moral questions; he would inculcate principles of virtue and benevolence. With such views he visited Dublin, scattered abroad a couple of pamphlets, spoke at a public meeting where O'Connell had harangued, dined with Curran and felt no liking for his host, discovered that the state of Irish politics and parties was not quite as simple as he had supposed, and, yielding to Godwin's advice and his own sense of failure, quitted Ireland, having effected little for the cause in which he was interested.

From Dublin Shelley, with Harriet and the inevitable Eliza Westbrook, crossed to Wales, and, after a short residence amid wood and stream and mountain at Nantgwillt, proceeded to the coast of North Devon, and took up his abode (June, 1812) in a cottage at Lynmouth, then a secluded fishing-village. The July and August days were among the happiest of Shelley's life; his regard for his young wife had deepened into sincere love; he was in communication with the immortal Godwin; his lady of light, Miss Hitchener, visited the

Introduction

cottage, and was not yet discovered to be an intolerable affliction; his mind was vigorously occupied with a prose pleading on behalf of liberty of speech, — the "Letter to Lord Ellenborough," — and with certain ambitious enterprises in verse. Of these last some still remain in manuscript; but the most important, "Queen Mab," sufficiently exposes its author's spirit at this period, his convictions, his hopes, his dreams, his views of the past, his aspirations toward the future. "It is," I have said elsewhere, "a kind of synthesis which harmonizes the political and social fervours of the Irish expedition, with all their wisdom and folly, and the imaginative exaltation to which the grandeur and loveliness of Welsh hillsides and Devon cliffs and waves had given rise." It is a pamphlet in verse, but with some of the beauty of poetry underlying its declamatory prophesyings. Its pictorial effects are sometimes rather spectacular than in a high sense imaginative. Its thought is often crude. It suffers from a moral shallowness, derived in part from Godwin, and arising from the supposition that evil exists less in human character than in human institutions. Its survey of the past history of society is superficial and one-sided ; its hopes for the future are in great part fantastic. Yet the poem, which may be held to lie midway between Shelley's " Juvenilia " and the works of his adult years, has value in its deep sympathy with humanity and its imaginative setting forth of the idea of a cosmos, the unity of nature, the universality of law, the vast and ceaseless flow of Being ever subject to a process of evolution and development. In certain passages the writer ceases to be a doctrinaire rhetorician, and rises into a poet who can interpret alike the facts of external nature and the longings of the human heart "Villainous trash," was Shelley's own description of " Queen Mab," when a pirated edition appeared in 1821; but time, the arbiter, has pronounced that it forms in fact an integral part of his gift to our literature. " Queen Mab " was finished in February, 1813, and was printed in that year for private distribution.

Shelley's residence at Lynmouth came to an untimely end. He had amused himself — yet with a grave face — by launching into the Bristol Channel boxes and bottles, each laden

Introduction

with a copy of his broadsheet " Declaration of Rights," or his poem " The Devil's Walk," for the waves and winds to put into circulation. On 19th August his Irish servant was watched as he posted up about Barnstaple copies of the " Declaration," a statement on the subject of government and society drawn up on the model of French Revolutionary documents. The Irishman was arrested, convicted, and sentenced to six months' imprisonment. His master, having done what he could to lighten Dan's sufferings in prison, hastily left the Lynmouth cottage, and took refuge in the little town of Tremadoc in the county of Carnarvon. Here for a time Shelley was much interested in the fortunes of the great embankment, designed to rescue a tract of land from the sea. He attempted to collect funds to carry on the undertaking, contributed himself out of all proportion to his means, and visited London in order to solicit further subscriptions. In London (October, 1812) he saw Godwin face to face for the first time, and the impression on each side was favourable. He renewed his friendship with Hogg; finally broke with his once worshipped, now detested, Miss Hitchener; and added to the circle of his acquaintances the agreeable family of Mr. Newton, whose zeal on behalf of vegetarianism commended him to Shelley. During the winter in Wales he exerted himself generously on behalf of the suffering poor; he studied the philosophers of the French illumination, and, under Godwin's advice, endeavoured to gain some real acquaintance with history, added to his store of manuscript poems, and prepared for publication a series of extracts from the Bible which were selected with a view to set forth a pure morality unencumbered by what Shelley held to be Biblical mythology. On the night of 26th February, 1813, the lonely house of Tanyrallt, which the Shelleys occupied, was entered by some villain bent on outrage. Alarmed by the noise, Shelley descended, pistols in hand, from his bedroom. Shots were fired and an encounter took place, which ended in the escape of the marauder. Attempts have been made to discredit the story of this adventure. There do not appear to be sufficient grounds for disbelief, but we may perhaps accept the theory that Shelley's overwrought nerves played tricks upon him after the attack,

Introduction

and that the alleged later attempt at assassination on the same night was a delusion of the brain.

On a second visit to Ireland Shelley travelled as far south as Killarney and Cork. In April he was again in London, where in June, 1813, his first child, a girl, named Ianthe, was born. "He was extremely fond of his child," says Peacock, "and would walk up and down a room with it in his arms for a long time together, singing to it a monotonous melody of his own making." When Harriet had recovered, she and her husband moved to Bracknell in Berkshire, attracted thither by the presence of Mrs. Boinville (sister-in-law of the vegetarian Newton) and her young married daughter, Cornelia Turner. These new friends were cultivated, refined, enthusiastic, perhaps somewhat sentimental. With Cornelia as his fellow student Shelley made progress in Ariosto, Tasso, Petrarch. It would have been a time of great enjoyment but that pecuniary troubles disturbed him; debts had accumulated, and he was forced to raise money at ruinous interest by post-obit bonds. In October he left Bracknell, wandered northward to the English lakes, and thence proceeded to Edinburgh. But his stay in Scotland was not for long. Before the close of the year he was settled in a furnished house at Windsor, in the midst of his school-boy haunts and at no great distance from Brack-nell, where the Boinvilles still resided. For a time he occupied himself in writing the dialogue published in 1814 with the title, "A Refutation of Deism," in which it is his aim to demon-strate that no *via media* can be found between Christianity and Atheism.

In order to raise money it was necessary to place beyond all doubt the legitimacy of any son and heir who might be born to Shelley; doubts were probably raised as to the validity of the Scotch wedding; and accordingly, on 24th March, 1814, Shelley went through the ceremony of marriage with Harriet according to the rites of the Church of England. But before this event his domestic happiness had been grievously clouded. Whatever intellectual and spiritual sympathy at any time existed between him and his young wife had now ceased to exist. She aspired to a more fashionable life than he could endure; her expenditure on dress, silver plate, and a carriage plunged him

Introduction

deeper in debt, when debt had become a misery and a degradation. Eliza Westbrook had grown an intolerable presence in the household, and yet Eliza Westbrook was for ever at hand. Shelley was urgent that Harriet should nurse her child, and Harriet insisted on hiring a wet-nurse. At length the managing elder sister withdrew, but Harriet maintained after her departure a hard and cold bearing as of one who had suffered wrong. Shelley sought for some imperfect consolation in the friendship of Mrs. Boinville and Mrs. Turner. In May he implored for a reconciliation, but without effect. Harriet quitted her home and went to reside in Bath, while her husband took refuge in London.

With characteristic generosity he was at this time endeavouring to succour Godwin, who had pressing need of a large sum of money. In May or June Shelley first looked with interest on Mary, the daughter of Godwin and Mary Wollstonecraft. She had just returned from a visit to Scotland — a girl in her seventeenth year, with golden hair, a pale, pure face, great forehead, and earnest eyes of hazel. She was vigorous of intellect, possessed of much mental courage and much firmness of will, united with

Introduction

sensibility and ardour of heart. The second Mrs. Godwin had made Mary's home unhappy. She and Shelley drew toward each other in what at first seemed to be friendship, but quickly proved itself love. At the same time—if we may trust a statement of Mrs. Godwin's daughter, Claire Clairmont—Shelley had not only come to believe that Harriet had ceased to love him; he declared his belief that she had proved faithless to him, and had formed a connection with an Irish officer named Ryan. There is no proof that Shelley had evidence sufficient to support this charge, and Harriet herself asserted her fidelity. Her assertion is supported by Thornton Hunt, Hookham, Hogg, and others. But Godwin stated in 1817 that he knew from unquestionable authority, wholly unconnected with Shelley, that Harriet had proved unfaithful to her husband before their separation. We can readily suppose that Shelley might persuade himself of what was not the fact. He wrote to Harriet begging her to come to London. On her arrival (14th July) he told her that he could no longer regard her as his wife; that his heart was given to Mary Godwin; but that he would continue, as far as might be, to watch over her interests. The shock and agitation of Shelley's disclosure brought an illness on Harriet, during which Eliza West-brook was in constant attendance, and Shelley besought the sufferer to return to life and health. But his resolution to part from her remained unchanged. Having made arrangements for Harriet's material comfort, he prepared, without the knowledge of Godwin or his wife, for flight with Mary. On the morning of 28th July, 1814, the fugitives were on their way to France. They had persuaded Claire Clairmont, the daughter of Godwin's wife by a previous marriage, to be their companion. An idealised record of Shelley's days of misery with Harriet is probably to be found in the confessions of the madhouse-prisoner of "Julian and Maddalo." A less obscure narrative of the causes of estrangement is given with altered names in Mrs. Shelley's novel of "Lodore."

Crossing from Dover to Calais in an open boat, the runaways made for Paris, and having there procured money, they travelled, Shelley on foot, Mary or Claire on muleback, toward

Introduction

Switzerland. From Troyes Shelley wrote to Harriet a letter which would be incomprehensible if coming from any other writer, in which he expressed a hope that she would follow them, and reside under his care in their immediate neighbourhood. On reaching Brunnen on the Lake of Lucerne, the wanderers engaged rooms, but apprehending a difficulty of obtaining supplies at so great a distance from England, they hastily turned homewards, descended the Rhine as far as Cologne, and after an absence of six weeks reached London in the middle of September.

The months in London between mid-September and January, 1815, were months of trial and vexation. Godwin was estranged; the intercourse with Harriet, who in November gave birth to Shelley's second child, a son, was of a troubled kind; there were sore straits for money, and during some days Shelley, while hiding from creditors, was parted from Mary. But the opening month of 1815 altered his circumstances. On 6th January his grandfather died, and Shelley became the immediate heir to a great property. By parting with his interest in a portion of the estates to his father, he secured an annual income of one thousand pounds, and also received a considerable sum for the payment of his debts. Unhappily, at the same time that his worldly goods increased, his health in some degree failed. In the summer he wandered through Devon, and early in August found a happy resting-place at Bishopsgate, on the borders of Windsor Park. Accompanied by Mary and his friend Peacock, he spent some delightful days in a river excursion up the Thames as far as Lechlade, of which we have a memorial in one of the early lyrical pieces. On his return home he composed in the glades of Windsor Great Park the poem which first proves that his genius had attained to adult years, his "Alastor." It is, in its inmost sense, a pleading on behalf of human love — that love which he had himself sought and found; it is a rebuke to the man of genius — the seeker for beauty and the seeker for truth — who would live apart from human sympathy; yet the fate of the solitary idealist, Shelley tells us, is less mournful than that of one who should fatten in apathy, "instigated by no sacred thirst of doubtful knowledge, duped by no illustrious superstition."

Introduction

The poem is a record, marvellously exalted, of his experiences of the past year, — his thoughts of love and death, and the impressions derived from external nature amid Swiss lake and mountain, on the arrowy Reuss, among the rock-guarded passes of the Rhine, and in presence of the autumnal glories of Windsor Forest.

In January, 1816, Mary gave birth to a boy, named William after her father. Still Godwin maintained his attitude of alienation from Shelley, though he deigned to accept liberal gifts of money. At length Shelley grew indignant, yet was not the less zealous in rendering Godwin what aid he could. It seemed that Mary and he would be happier in any other country than in England, where kinsfolk and former friends averted their faces in anger or in shame. Accordingly, it was decided that trial should be made of a residence abroad; there would be a compensation in the diminished cost of living for the loss of English fields and skies. In the early days of May, 1816, Shelley, with Mary, little William, and Claire Clairmont, was *en route* for Geneva by way of Paris.

Introduction

Of Byron's intrigue with Miss Clairmont, Shelley and Mary, when they started from England, were in profound ignorance. But it was with a view of meeting Byron that Claire had been urgent with Shelley to take her abroad. At Sécheron, a small suburb of Geneva, the two great poets met. When Shelley moved into occupation of a cottage on the opposite side of the lake, and Byron took refuge from an importunate public at the Villa Diodati, they were in constant communication. They rowed or sailed together, and toward the close of June circumnavigated the lake, during which excursion "The Prisoner of Chillon" was written. With Mary for his companion, Shelley visited Chamouni. The feelings with which Swiss scenery inspired him may be read in the poem, "Mont Blanc," and the noble "Hymn to Intellectual Beauty." Mary also was moved to imaginative creation, and now conceived the design of her tale of "Frankenstein," undertaken in fulfilment of an agreement that each of the friends — herself, Byron, Shelley, and the young physician, Polidori — should produce a ghost story, Notwithstanding the delights of Switzerland, the

Introduction

hearts of Shelley and Mary turned longingly toward England. Before quitting Geneva they had the pleasure of making the acquaintance of M. G. Lewis, the celebrated author of " The Monk," a book which Shelley, as a boy, had read with eager enjoyment. Early in September their feet were once more on English soil.

But it seemed as if they had returned only to encounter calamity. On 9th October Mary's half-sister, Fanny, the daughter of Mary Wollstonecraft, who had been for some time past in depressed spirits, put an end to her life by poison at an inn in Swansea. Alarmed by a desponding letter, Shelley had hastened from Bath, where he was residing, to meet her, but arrived too late. The shock of excitement and grief was for a time disastrous to his health, and it was well for him that at this moment he found a friend of bright and courageous temper in Leigh Hunt. Disaster, however, followed on disaster. In November Shelley was seeking to discover Harriet, who had disappeared from his ken and from the protection of her father. On 10th December her body was found in the Serpentine River.

Introduction

At first after the parting with Shelley she had hoped that he would return to her; when this hope faded away her unhappiness was great, she complained of the restraint to which she was subjected in her father's house, and already spoke of suicide. For some time before her death she had broken away from that restraint. Her daughter, aged three, and her little boy of two years old, had been placed with a clergyman in Warwick. She herself lived openly for a time, Godwin tells a correspondent, with a certain colonel whom he names. Then she seems to have sunk lower, and to have been deserted. In informing Shelley of the terrible event, the bookseller, Hookham, mentions that had she lived a little longer she would have given birth to a child.[1] The evidence at the coroner's inquest confirms the statement. Shelley was deeply moved, but not as though he were the author of the calamity. "I take

---

[1] When I wrote my "Life of Shelley," I did not think it necessary to state some of the facts mentioned above, with the result that some critics, who did not take the trouble to examine *The Times* newspaper to which I referred, charged me with making false accusations against Harriet Shelley, whose faults I desired not to deny but to veil. Since then Mrs. Marshall has set forth the facts in her "Life and Letters of Mary Wollstonecraft Shelley," and I have now no motive for reserve

Introduction

God to witness, if such a Being is now regarding both you and me," he afterward wrote to Southey, "and I pledge myself, if we meet, as perhaps you expect, before Him after death, to repeat the same in His presence — that you accuse me wrongfully. I am innocent of ill, either done or intended." It was now possible for him to give Mary her right name of wife, and he lost no time in celebrating his marriage (30th December, 1816). He claimed his children from the Westbrooks, but the claim was resisted. After tedious proceedings in Chancery, judgment was given by Lord Eldon to the effect that, inasmuch as Shelley's professed opinions led to conduct which the law pronounced immoral, the children could not be placed in his immediate care; but since he had named suitable persons to educate them — a Doctor and Mrs. Hume — they should be entrusted to these custodians during their minority, and the father should be permitted at certain times to see them. The chancellor's decision was not designed to be harsher than seemed necessary; but the loss of his children was a greater blow to Shelley than the death of their mother, and for a time he even feared that little William might also be taken from him.

While the Chancery affair was proceeding, Shelley resided at Great Marlow, on the Thames. Occasionally in London he visited Hunt, at whose house he met Keats and Hazlitt. He was now on amicable terms with Godwin, and gained a new and valuable friend in Horace Smith. At Marlow, notwithstanding the Chancery troubles, he had many happy days; he read much in classical and modern literature; designed and wrote some portions of " Prince Athanase" and of " Rosalind and Helen;" and while alone in his boat on the Thames or among the Bisham woods, he made steady progress with his ambitious epic of revolution and counter-revolution, " Laon and Cythna." " He saw, or thought he saw" — I quote words of my own previously written — " as the great fact of the age a vast movement toward the reconstruction of society, in which the French Revolution had been a startling incident — an incident fruitful of much evil and much good. It was his desire to rekindle in men the aspiration toward a happier condition of moral and political society, and

at the same time to warn men of the dangers
which arise in a movement of revolution from
their own egoisms and greeds and baser passions; it was his desire to present the true
ideal of revolution — a national movement
based on moral principle, inspired by justice
and charity, unstained by blood, unclouded by
turbulence, and using material force only as the
tranquil putting forth in act of spiritual powers.
. . . Unhappily, with all that was admirable
in the revolutionary movement of his time, —
its enthusiasm of humanity, its recognition of
a moral element in politics, its sentiment
of the brotherhood of man, — there are united
in Shelley's poem all its shallow sophisms.
Shelley's illusions are such as could now deceive
no thinking mind. His generous ardours, the
quivering music of his verse, the quick and
flamelike beauty of his imagery, still bear gifts
for the spirits of men."

Some few copies of " Laon and Cythna "
had been issued when voices of protest alarmed
Ollier the publisher. He insisted that certain
alterations should be made. Violent attacks
on theism and the Christian faith, as he held,
were ill-judged and out of place; the relation-

ship of the hero and heroine as brother and sister was a ground of grave and just offence. And it is true that in this last particular Shelley's poem gave a flagrant example of the unsoundness of the revolutionary way of thought, which with a solvent of abstract notions, erroneously deduced, proceeds to disintegrate social relations and sentiments that are among the finest products of the evolution of the race. By some strokes of the pen and a few cancel-pages " Laon and Cythna " was altered into " The Revolt of Islam." There was the loss of one or two admirable lines ; but in yielding to the pressure of public feeling, acting through his publisher, Shelley removed an ethical blot which could not fail with many, and those not the least judicious, readers, to mar even the artistic effect of his poem.

During the early months of 1817, the effects of a bad harvest were keenly felt by the poor of Marlow, where lace-making was the principal industry. Shelley, says Peacock, went continually among them, and to the extent of his ability relieved the most urgent cases of distress. He organized his relief into a system, and among those in need gave a preference to widows and children. The wrongs and sufferings of the toiling masses weighed heavily on his spirit. Yet in "A Proposal for Putting Reform to the Vote," by "The Hermit of Marlow," he showed himself more moderate in his demands of immediate reform than many of his political contemporaries. This, indeed, was characteristic of Shelley. He was opposed to violence, and was well content with small gains as an instalment, though his vision of the remote future never permitted him to rest in any provisional advantage. Shelley's poetry expresses his visions as a seer of the far-off golden age; his prose writings express his thoughts as a practical reformer. In "An Address to the People on the Death of the Princess Charlotte," he laments the death of the young wife and mother; but he sees a more grievous calamity, and one worthy of deeper grief, in the condition of the people of England. Shelley's labours among the poor, his anxiety in connection with the Chancery affair, and the excitement of poetical composition injuriously affected his health. It was even feared that seeds of consumption were being developed in his constitution. He

Introduction

resolved to leave Marlow, which evidently did not suit him, and make the experiment of a residence in Italy. Another motive tended to draw him in that direction — Byron was at Venice, and Shelley desired that Byron's daughter, Allegra, the child of Miss Clairmont, should be placed under her father's care. The mother, not without misgivings, consented. On 12th March Shelley looked for the last time on English skies and fields. Accompanied by Mary, little William, his infant daughter Clara (born 2d September, 1817), and Miss Clairmont with her child, Shelley sailed to Dover, travelled south, and, having crossed Mont Cenis, reached Milan by the 4th of April, 1818.

Shelley had hoped to settle on the shores of Como, but a suitable residence could not be found. Pisa and Leghorn were successively visited. In the latter city resided Mr. and Mrs. Gisborne, with the son of Mrs. Gisborne by a previous marriage, Henry Reveley, a young engineer. Mrs. Gisborne had been an old and valued friend of Godwin; she was a woman of fine character — sensitive, modest, cultivated, with much intellectual curiosity; it was indeed a piece of good fortune to find such an acquaintance in a strange land. The summer was spent delightfully at the baths of Lucca, under green chestnut boughs, and within hearing of the Lima dashing upon its rocks. During these midsummer weeks Shelley wrote his translation of Plato's " Banquet," — a rendering which has much of the luminous beauty of the original. To please Mary he took up his unfinished " Rosalind and Helen," begun at Marlow, and quickly carried it to the close. This poem, partly suggested by circumstances in the life of Mary's friend, Isabel Booth (born Baxter), was published, together with the " Lines Written Among the Euganean Hills," the " Hymn to Intellectual Beauty," and the sonnet " Ozymandias," in the spring of 1819.

Desirous to see her child Allegra, Miss Clairmont visited Venice in August, with Shelley as her companion of the way. It was proposed in a friendly mood by Byron that Shelley and his family should occupy his villa at Este, among the Euganean hills, and that Miss Clairmont should there for a time enjoy companionship with Allegra. The proposal

Introduction

was gladly accepted. Mary arrived with her children at Este, but little Clara was seriously ill. It was necessary to consult a physician at Venice; unfortunately the passport had been forgotten, but Shelley's impetuosity overcame the resistance of the soldiers. The anxious parents reached Venice on 24th September, only to learn that there was no hope, and within an hour little Clara lay dead in her mother's arms.

Shelley's impressions of Venice and of Byron at this period may be found in his letters and in the admirable poem, "Julian and Maddalo." The letters exhibit the coarser side of Byron's Venetian life. In the poem is given a portrait of Byron, drawn without the baser lines and darker colours. The incidents there recorded — the ride on the Lido, the glory of sunset, viewed from the gondola's covert, the visit to the dreary island of the bell and tower, the sight of Allegra in her bright childhold — are probably idealized from recollection of what had actually taken place. In the story of the maniac, Shelley interweaves memories of his own unhappy past.

Greater designs, however, occupied his

thoughts, — a tragedy of " Tasso " (of which
we possess some fragments), a lyrical drama on
a subject derived from the Book of Job, and
the " Prometheus Unbound." In the summer-
house at Este the first act of " Prometheus "
was almost completed by the first days of October, 1818. The fortitude of a heroic saviour
of mankind, with his final victory, was a theme
which interested Shelley's deepest feelings, and
aroused the noblest powers of his imagination.

A warmer climate for the winter than that
of North Italy seemed desirable, and in November Shelley and his family journeyed to
the south. The greatness of antique Rome,
as seen in its monuments, impressed him
deeply, and he began a tale of the Coliseum,
which, however, was never finished. But he
had chosen Naples as his place of winter residence, and thither before the close of November he pursued his way. No prose writings
in our language are more instinct with radiance
and beauty than Shelley's letters which tell of
his visit to Pompeii, Vesuvius, Pæstum. Reminiscences of the day at Pompeii appear in the
" Ode to Naples," written two years later. Yet
it is certain that Shelley's spirits often drooped

during his stay at Naples, and this melancholy mood found poetical expression in one of the most pathetic of his lyrical pieces. In the spring of 1819 he returned to Rome, saw the ceremonies of Holy Week, and studied classical sculpture and Renaissance paintings. The second and third acts of " Prometheus Unbound " were written among the ruins of the Baths of Caracalla, then overgrown with flowers and blossoming shrubs. " The blue sky of Rome," he writes, " and the effect of the vigorous awakening of spring in that divinest climate, and the new life with which it drenches the spirit even to intoxication, were the inspiration of this drama." The fourth act — a sublime afterthought — was added in December, 1819, at Florence.

The days at Rome were darkened in June by the greatest sorrow of Shelley's later years. On the 7th of that month his beloved son William died; the father had watched during sixty hours of agony. In the English burial-ground, near the Porta San Paola, the little body was laid to rest. Mary's anguish was extreme, all her happiness seemed to be for ever lost. In order that she might have Mrs.

Introduction

Gisborne's companionship, a little country house, the Villa Valsovano, at a short distance from Leghorn, was taken for three months, and here, in the glazed terrace at the top of the house, Shelley studied, meditated, and basked in the summer sunshine. The tragedy of "The Cenci," begun at Rome, and interrupted by the death of his son, now advanced rapidly. The exhibition of tyrannous power, in the person of the count, and of martyr energy in Beatrice, born for gentleness and love, was admirably suited to the genius of Shelley. While essentially real and human, the drama moves among ideal passions. Horror is here ennobled by beauty, as Shelley himself describes it in his stanzas suggested by the Medusa of Leonardo da Vinci. A small edition of his tragedy was struck off in quarto at Leghorn and was sent to England to be sold by the Olliers.

But the work of Shelley's *annus mirabilis*, 1819, was not yet complete. At Florence, whither in October he had removed from the summer residence near Leghorn, he made notes upon the sculptures in the galleries. At the same time he did not forget England,

and its social and political needs. In the unfinished "Philosophical View of Reform" he attempted to investigate the causes of the distress of the English people, and to suggest the proper remedies. Tidings of the so-called "Manchester Massacre" affected Shelley deeply, and led him to write the admirable "Mask of Anarchy," in which he exhorts his countrymen to ways of peace and soberness — the true ways which lead to liberty. In the fantastic satire, "Peter Bell the Third," Wordsworth, turned a Tory, is taken as a type of the self-betrayal of genius to the stultifying influences of the world; the poem is an example, not altogether happy, of Shelley's handling of the humourous-grotesque. The great "Ode to the West Wind," in which there is a union of lyrical breadth with lyrical intensity unsurpassed in English song, was conceived and partly written in a wood that skirted the Arno on a day when the autumnal gale was gathering the vapours and rain-clouds, but to Shelley's imagination the wild wind of autumn becomes a harbinger of spring. Finally, in hours when he did not feel himself capable of creative work, he translated into graceful

English verse Euripides' drama of "The Cyclops." Assuredly no greater gift to English poetry was ever given by a poet within a twelvemonth than Shelley's gift of 1819.

At Florence on 12th November the son who survived his father, and who was to comfort his mother in her sorrows, Percy Florence, was born. As winter advanced, Shelley, suffering from the severe climate, decided to migrate to Pisa, where the air was mild, the water singularly pure, and an eminent physician, Vaccà Berlinghieri, might be consulted. The greater part of his life, from January, 1820, to the close, was spent in Pisa. The presence of Mr. Tighe and Lady Mountcashell (a former pupil of Mary Wollstonecraft) added to the attractions of the place. In the summer of 1820 a move was made to the Gisbornes' house at Leghorn, then unoccupied. And here was written that most delightful of poetical epistles, the letter to Maria Gisborne. Mary had in part recovered her spirits, and little Percy was "the merriest babe in the world." The mother was not wholly occupied with domestic cares, for she threw herself with spirit into the study of

Introduction

Greek, while Shelley occupied himself with the holiday task, so happily executed, of translating the Homeric "Hymn to Mercury" into *ottava rima*. As the heats grew more trying, they took refuge at the Baths of San Giuliano, some four miles distant from Pisa. During an expedition to Monte San Pellegrino, the resort of pilgrims at certain seasons of the year, Shelley conceived the idea of the "Witch of Atlas;" the poem was written in the three days which immediately succeeded his return to the Baths. It would have pleased Mary better if he had chosen a theme less remote from human sympathy; she playfully reproached him, and her faultfinding drew forth the graceful rejoinder which may be read in the introductory stanzas. When a little later he dealt in a grotesque manner with events of contemporary history, the result was by no means so fortunate; "Œdipus Tyrannus, or Swellfoot the Tyrant," which dramatizes, with satirical intention, the affair of Queen Caroline, is among the least happy of its author's efforts, yet it has a certain value as presenting a curious facet of his mind. "Swellfoot" was published in Lon-

Introduction

don in 1820, but was almost immediately
withdrawn from circulation by the publisher.

In the autumn (1820) Shelley, with his wife
and infant son, returned to Pisa. They had
been relieved of the presence of Miss Clairmont, who had taken a situation as governess
at Florence; but Shelley corresponded with
her, and took the kindest interest in all that
concerned her. Friends and acquaintances
gathered around him at Pisa, — his cousin and
former schoolfellow, Thomas Medwin, now a
captain of dragoons, lately returned from India;
the Irishman, Count Taaffe, who regarded himself as laureate of the city, and a learned critic
of Italian literature; Sgricci, the celebrated
improvvisatore; and Prince Mavrocordato,
son of the ex-hospodar of Wallachia, young,
ardent, cultured, who was to become the foremost statesman of the Greek Revolution.
Through a sometime professor of physics at
the University of Pisa, Francesco Pacchiani,
Shelley was introduced to Emelia, the daughter of Count Viviani, who had been confined
for two years in the Convent of St. Anna.
Mary and Shelley were both deeply interested in the beautiful Italian girl. Her youth,

her charm, her sorrows, awoke in Shelley all
the idealizing power of his imagination; she
became to him, as it were, a symbol of all that
is radiant and divine, all that is to be pursued
and never attained, — the absolute of beauty,
truth, and love. While for the man she was
a living and breathing woman, fascinating, and
an object of tenderest solicitude, for the poet
she rose into the avatar of the ideal. With
such a feeling toward Emelia he wrote his
"Epipsychidion." "It is," he tells Mr. Gisborne, "a mystery; as to real flesh and blood,
you know I do not deal in these articles. . . .
I desired Ollier not to circulate this piece except to the συνετοί, and even they, it seems,
are inclined to approximate me to the circle
of a servant-girl and her sweetheart." As had
happened so often before, Shelley, in due time,
passed out of his idealizing mood. "The
Epipsychidion," he afterward wrote, "I cannot look at; the person whom it celebrates
was a cloud instead of a Juno; and poor Ixion
starts from the centaur that was the offspring
of his own embrace." The same idealizing
ardour which found poetical expression in
"Epipsychidion," gave its elevated tone to

Introduction

Shelley's essay in criticism, the "Defence of Poetry," written in February and March, 1821, as a reply to Peacock's "Four Ages of Poetry." It is perhaps the most admirable of his prose writings, and serves as an undesigned exposition of the processes of his own mind as an imaginative creator.

The summer of 1821, like that of the preceding year, was spent at the Baths of San Giuliano. A friendship had sprung up in Pisa between Shelley and a young half-pay lieutenant of dragoons, Edward Williams, who, with his wife, had been attracted to Italy partly by Medwin's promise that he should be introduced to Shelley. The Williamses had taken a charming villa four miles from Shelley's residence at the Baths, and communication was easy and delightful by means of a boat on the canal which was fed by the waters of the Serchio. Edward Williams was frank, simple, kind-hearted, and not without a lively interest in literature; Jane had a sweet insinuating grace, and could gratify Shelley's ear with the melodies of her guitar. The days passed happily, and might have passed without a memorable incident save for an event not im-

mediately connected with the dwellers at the
Baths. In February, 1821, occurred the death
of Keats at Rome; but tidings did not reach
Shelley until April. He had known Keats,
but had never felt a deep personal affection for
him. The genius of the young poet, however,
was honoured by Shelley, who, on hearing of
his illness in the summer of 1820, had invited
him to Pisa. Deeply moved, through his
imagination rather than his affections, by the
story of the death of Keats, Shelley did homage
to his memory in the elegy of " Adonais,"
which takes its place in literature beside the
laments of Moschus for Bion and of Milton
for Lycidas. Before its close the poem rises
into an impassioned hymn not of death but of
immortal life.

The pleasure of a visit to Byron at Ravenna
in August was more than marred by Byron's
sudden disclosure of certain shocking accusations which had been brought against Shelley
in his domestic life. An ardent letter of vin-
dication, to be forwarded by Byron to the English consul at Venice, was written by Mary;
but it never reached Mr. Hoppner, for whom
it was intended, and was found among Byron's

Introduction

papers after his death. "That my beloved
Shelley should stand thus slandered in your
minds," so Mary wrote, "he the gentlest and
most humane of creatures — is more painful to
me, oh! far more painful than words can express." If they could but escape to some solitude far from the world and its calumnies! Or,
since this was impossible, if they could gather
around them in their Pisan home a little circle
of true and loyal friends! Of these Byron —
it was hoped — might be one, for he was about
to quit Ravenna, and he desired them to hire a
house for himself and the Countess Guiccioli at
Pisa. Leigh Hunt, at home in England, had
for some time past been seriously ill; he also
might form one of their company, and the new
periodical, *The Liberal*, of which there had been
talk, might be started for his benefit by the
literary coalition.

"I am full of thoughts and plans," Shelley
wrote to Hunt in August, 1821. Not one of
his larger designs was achieved, but in the
summer or early autumn of that year he rapidly
produced his "Hellas," remarkable as an idealized treatment of contemporary events. In
the "Persæ" of Æschylus he found a precedent

lviii

and to some extent a model for his poetic dealing with current facts. The phantom of Mahomet II. is suggested by the figure of Darius in the "Persians;" but instead of the ode of lamentation which closes the Greek play, the lyrical prophecy with which "Hellas" ends is a song of joy and love for the whole world.

"Lord Byron is established here," Shelley wrote from Pisa in January, 1822, "and we are constant companions." They rode together; practised pistol-shooting or played billiards; interchanged their views on literary and social questions. Shelley felt toward Byron as toward a great creative power, which subdued him to admiration; yet there were times when he was repelled by proofs of the coarser fibre of Byron's moral nature. The opening year brought a new acquaintance to Pisa,—Edward John Trelawny, a young Cornish gentleman, who had led a life of various adventure by sea and land. Trelawny, "with his knight-errant aspect, dark, handsome, and mustachioed," interested Shelley and Mary more than any acquaintance whom they had made since the departure of Mavrocordato. How Shelley charmed Trelawny may be read in the delightful " Recollections " of the latter, which give us the most vivid image of the poet in the closing months of his life. Trelawny, Williams, and Shelley were lovers of the sea. It was agreed that a boat should be built, and that a seaside house should be taken for the summer at Spezzia. Meanwhile Shelley worked now and again at his historical play of " Charles I.," and wrote some of those exquisite lyrical poems inspired by the grace and subtle attraction of Jane Williams, the wife of his young and bright-tempered companion.

Casa Magni, the house taken for the summer migrants, stands on the margin of the sea, near the fishing-village of San Terenzo, on the eastern side of the Bay of Spezzia. The first days were saddened by a grief to all, but in a special degree a grief to Miss Clairmont — the death at the convent of Bagnacavallo of little Allegra. Mary was in delicate health, and found the lonely house by the sea oppressive to her spirits. Shelley's overwrought nerves conjured up visionary forms : on one occasion the figure of Allegra rose smiling upon him from the moonlit sea, clapping its hands for joy. But when the long-expected boat rounded the point of Porto Venere all was gladness and bustle of expectation. "We have now," wrote Williams, who with Jane occupied a part of Casa Magni, "a perfect plaything for the summer." While during the heats of the June days Shelley rested in his boat, or gazed from shore on the splendours of the sea, or on moonlight nights sat among the rocks, he wrote the noble fragments of his last great unfinished poem, "The Triumph of Life." It contains perhaps the wisest thoughts of his whole life; it expresses a mood of pathetic renunciation, with insight reached after error, and serenity attained through passion. In its general design and in the form of verse it follows Petrarch's "Triumph of Love;" in the details of its imagery it sometimes approaches the manner of Dante.

The return to Casa Magni of Claire, after a couple of weeks' absence, was almost immediately followed by a calamity which threatened serious risk to Mary's life — a dangerous miscarriage. By Shelley's energy and promptitude her life was saved; but the strain upon his nerves again caused him to be troubled by frequent visions. On 19th June news came which

Introduction

rejoiced his heart — Leigh Hunt and his family
had arrived in Italy.   It was glorious midsummer weather; the boat, with Shelley and Williams on board, was put to sea, and after a
prosperous run anchor was cast in the port of
Leghorn.   Next morning the long-parted
friends, Hunt and Shelley, met.   " I am inexpressibly delighted," cried Shelley, " you cannot think how inexpressibly happy it makes
me."   " He was looking better," wrote Hunt,
" than I had ever seen him ; we talked of a
thousand things — we anticipated a thousand
pleasures."   On Monday, 8th July, the aspect
of the sky seemed to portend a change of
weather; but the breeze was favourable for a
return to Lerici.   Between one and two o'clock
the boat left the harbour.   It was observed
about ten miles out at sea, off Via Reggio;
then the haze of a summer storm hid it from
view.

Meanwhile Mary, who had been loath to
allow Shelley to leave her, and Jane Williams
watched and waited.   Days of misery and
dreadful suspense went by.   At length the
widowed women could endure it no longer,
and posted to Pisa to make inquiries of Byron

and Hunt. Even then all hope was not extinct; the boat might have been blown to Corsica or Elba. Mary and Jane hastened back to Lerici, Trelawny having undertaken to renew the search in the direction of Leghorn. On the evening of 19th July he returned. "All was over," writes Mary; "all was quiet now; they had been found washed on shore."

Two bodies had been thrown upon the beach, one near Via Reggio, the other in Tuscan territory. The tall, slight figure, the volume of Sophocles, and Keats's poems identified the body of Shelley. According to the strict laws of Italian quarantine, the corpses should have remained under quicklime in the sands. But by special permission arrangements were made for their cremation. Trelawny, Byron, and Hunt were present. The heart of Shelley was snatched by Trelawny from the flames; the ashes were reverently collected. In the old Protestant burial-ground at Rome, where lay the body of Shelley's son, hard by the tomb of Caius Cestius, the casket containing the ashes was committed to the ground.

Mary Shelley survived her husband for nearly thirty years; she died on 21st Febru-

Introduction

ary, 1851. Charles Bysshe, the son of Shelley's first wife, died in early life. Shelley's last-born son, Percy Florence, succeeded to the baronetcy on the death of his grandfather in April, 1844. He died on 5th December, 1889. A monument to Shelley, by Weekes, is erected in the parish church of Christchurch, Hants. The relics, portraits, journals, manuscripts, and letters of Shelley and Mary, duly ordered by Lady Shelley's hands, are preserved at Boscombe Manor, near Bournemouth.

All who love Shelley's poetry are under inexpressible obligations to Mary Shelley, who gave to the world the great body of his posthumous writings, edited his works with loving care, though not with infallible accuracy, and added the inestimable memorials of his life, which may be read in her notes to the poems. Our debt is also great to three distinguished Shelley scholars: to Doctor Garnett, whose "Relics of Shelley," recovered from manuscripts which are often a tangle of corrections, form the most precious addition to Shelley's poetical works which has appeared since the publication of the Posthumous Poems, 1824; to Mr. W. M. Rossetti, and to Mr. Forman. Mr. Ros-

Introduction

setti increased the body of Shelley's published poetry by several pieces of value, and in particular added largely to the known fragments of Charles I. from a manuscript most difficult to decipher. His principles in dealing with the text led him to some changes which cannot be sustained, but in not a few instances he recovered the true text by happy emendation. Mr. Forman added to the published poems of Shelley the second part of the " Dæmon of the World," and some other pieces. His devotion to the author of his choice, his untiring zeal as a collector, his learning, his accuracy, his good judgment, have made him our chief living authority on all that relates to Shelley's writings. The present volume has gained much from Mr. Forman's labours; it is impossible but that it should be so. In its general plan, however, it differs materially from his editions, which reprint in chronological order the several volumes published during Shelley's life. In giving "The Revolt of Islam" rather than " Laon and Cythna," which Mr. Forman reprints, we follow the example of Mrs. Shelley; but in Notes to the present volume the readings of " Laon and Cythna" will be found. Mr. Forman's annotated edition is unquestionably that to which appeal must be made in any question of doubt on any point of Shelley scholarship. But perhaps if Mr. Rossetti modified the text of the early editions somewhat too freely, Mr. Forman has sometimes been overconservative of peculiarities of spelling and obvious errors of punctuation. When these cloud the sense, it seems permissible to make a correction in an edition designed for general use. Yet I should be slow to alter erroneous punctuation, if the meaning be not obscured, for such punctuation may have a metrical value. As to spelling, while in several instances (as "blosmy," "glode") it is desirable to preserve Shelley's spelling, it would be impossible, or at least intolerable, to follow his manuscripts in every instance ("thier" for "their," "mein" for "mien," etc.). A great poet is not of an age, but for all time. While texts of Shakespeare, Milton, and Pope, prepared for specialists, may rightly retain the peculiarities of the early editions, there must also be texts of Shakespeare, Milton, and Pope, in which every obstacle to the reader's pleasure, caused by the early printers, ought to be removed.

Introduction

All ascertained poems which have appeared in previous editions are included in the present volume. "The Wandering Jew" is not, and probably ought not, to be given as the work of Shelley. Two doubtful pieces — "The Dinner Party Anticipated, A Paraphrase of Horace's 19th Ode, B. III.," and "The Magic Horse, translated from the Italian of Cristofano Bronzino" (given in the appendix to Mr. Forman's library edition) — are excluded as of uncertain authorship A considerable body of Shelley's early verse existing in a manuscript book owned by the poet's grandson, Mr. Esdaile, remains unprinted. Mr. Esdaile, who kindly allowed me to print certain poems of biographical interest in my "Life of Shelley," has expressed his desire that they should not be now reprinted. It was, as he believes, the wish of Shelley's daughter Ianthe that the poems in this manuscript volume should not be included in an edition of her father's poetical works.

An arrangement of the poems differing somewhat from that of Mrs. Shelley has involved the displacing of a few paragraphs of her notes, so that these paragraphs may be read in connection with the poems to which they refer. In this particular the treatment of Mr. Rossetti has been adopted. The fragments of verse are placed among the poems of the years to which they respectively belong, as they have been placed by Mr. Forman, but in a somewhat different order. They have perhaps a better chance of being read with interest in such an arrangement as this than when they are massed together as a group by themselves. The titles of the shorter fragments are those of Mr. Forman, in cases where his titles seemed inevitably right, I have not felt at liberty to adopt his titles in other cases, and have proposed, for convenience of reference, titles of my own devising. Perhaps I have ventured too far in naming a fragment " Song of the Furies." A few notes, chiefly textual, are added at the end of the volume. In preparing these use has been made of Mr. Woodberry's " Notes on the MS. Volume of Shelley's Poems in the Library of Harvard College." A few corrections in the text of some of the " Juvenilia " are made from Shelley's manuscript.

I wish to express my thanks to Lady Shelley

Introduction

for favours which she has rendered in connection with this edition.   The portrait of Shelley
is from the likeness by Miss Curran in the
possession of Lady Shelley.

EDWARD DOWDEN.

Preface by Mrs. Shelley

OBSTACLES have long existed to my presenting the public with a perfect edition of Shelley's poems. These being at last happily removed, I hasten to fulfil an important duty, —that of giving the productions of a sublime genius to the world, with all the correctness possible, and of, at the same time, detailing the history of those productions, as they sprang, living and warm, from his heart and brain. I abstain from any remark on the occurrences of his private life, except inasmuch as the passions which they engendered inspired his poetry. This is not the time to relate the truth; and I should reject any colouring of the truth. No account of these events has ever been given at all approaching reality in their details, either as regards himself or others; nor shall I further allude to them than to remark that the errors of action

committed by a man as noble and generous as
Shelley may, as far as he only is concerned,
be fearlessly avowed by those who loved him,
in the firm conviction that, were they judged
impartially, his character would stand in fairer
and brighter light than that of any contemporary. Whatever faults he had ought to find
extenuation among his fellows, since they prove
him to be human; without them, the exalted
nature of his soul would have raised him into
something divine.

The qualities that struck any one newly
introduced to Shelley were, first, a gentle
and cordial goodness that animated his intercourse with warm affection and helpful sympathy; the other, the eagerness and ardour
with which he was attached to the cause of
human happiness and improvement, and the
fervent eloquence with which he discussed such
subjects. His conversation was marked by its
happy abundance and the beautiful language
in which he clothed his poetic ideas and philosophical notions. To defecate life of its misery
and its evil was the ruling passion of his soul;
he dedicated to it every power of his mind,
every pulsation of his heart. He looked on

Preface

political freedom as the direct agent to effect the happiness of mankind; and thus any new-sprung hope of liberty inspired a joy and an exultation more intense and wild than he could have felt for any personal advantage. Those who have never experienced the workings of passion on general and unselfish subjects cannot understand this; and it must be difficult of comprehension to the younger generation rising around, since they cannot remember the scorn and hatred with which the partisans of reform were regarded some few years ago, nor the persecutions to which they were exposed. He had been from youth the victim of the state of feeling inspired by the reaction of the French Revolution; and believing firmly in the justice and excellence of his views, it cannot be wondered that a nature as sensitive, as impetuous, and as generous as his should put its whole force into the attempt to alleviate for others the evils of those systems from which he had himself suffered. Many advantages attended his birth; he spurned them all when balanced with what he considered his duties. He was generous to imprudence, devoted to heroism.

Preface

These characteristics breathe throughout his poetry. The struggle for human weal ; the resolution firm to martyrdom ; the impetuous pursuit, the glad triumph in good ; the determination not to despair, — such were the features that marked those of his works which he regarded with most complacency, as sustained by a lofty subject and useful aim.

In addition to these, his poems may be divided into two classes, — the purely imaginative, and those which sprang from the emotions of his heart. Among the former may be classed the " Witch of Atlas," " Adonais," and his latest composition, left imperfect, the " Triumph of Life." In the first of these particularly he gave the reins to his fancy, and luxuriated in every idea as it rose; in all there is that sense of mystery which formed an essential portion of his perception of life — a clinging to the subtler inner spirit, rather than to the outward form — a curious and metaphysical anatomy of human passion and perception.

The second class is, of course, the more popular, as appealing at once to emotions common to us all ; some of these rest on the passion of love ; others on grief and despond-

Preface

ency; others on the sentiments inspired by
natural objects. Shelley's conception of love
was exalted, absorbing, allied to all that is
purest and noblest in our nature, and warmed
by earnest passion; such it appears when he
gave it a voice in verse. Yet he was usually
averse to expressing these feelings, except when
highly idealized; and many of his more beautiful effusions he had cast aside unfinished, and
they were never seen by me till after I had lost
him. Others, as for instance " Rosalind and
Helen" and "Lines Written Among the Euganean Hills," I found among his papers by
chance; and with some difficulty urged him to
complete them. There are others, such as the
" Ode to the Skylark " and " The Cloud,"
which, in the opinion of many critics, bear a
purer poetical stamp than any other of his
productions. They were written as his mind
prompted: listening to the carolling of the
bird, aloft in the azure sky of Italy; or mark-
ing the cloud as it sped across the heavens,
while he floated in his boat on the Thames.

No poet was ever warmed by a more genuine and unforced inspiration. His extreme
sensibility gave the intensity of passion to his

intellectual pursuits; and rendered his mind keenly alive to every perception of outward objects, as well as to his internal sensations. Such a gift is, among the sad vicissitudes of human life, the disappointments we meet, and the galling sense of our own mistakes and errors, fraught with pain; to escape from such, he delivered up his soul to poetry, and felt happy when he sheltered himself, from the influence of human sympathies, in the wildest regions of fancy. His imagination has been termed too brilliant, his thoughts too subtle. He loved to idealize reality; and this is a taste shared by few. We are willing to have our passing whims exalted into passions, for this gratifies our vanity; but few of us understand or sympathize with the endeavour to ally the love of abstract beauty and adoration of abstract good, the τὸ ἀγαθὸν καὶ τὸ καλόν of the Socratic philosophers, with our sympathies with our kind. In this, Shelley resembled Plato; both taking more delight in the abstract and the ideal than in the special and tangible. This did not result from imitation; for it was not till Shelley resided in Italy that he made Plato his study. He then translated his "Symposium" and his "Ion;" and the English language boasts of no more brilliant composition than Plato's "Praise of Love" translated by Shelley. To return to his own poetry. The luxury of imagination, which sought nothing beyond itself (as a child burdens itself with Spring flowers, thinking of no use beyond the enjoyment of gathering them), often showed itself in his verses: they will be only appreciated by minds which have resemblance to his own; and the mystic subtlety of many of his thoughts will share the same fate. The metaphysical strain that characterizes much of what he has written was, indeed, the portion of his works to which, apart from those whose scope was to awaken mankind to aspirations for what he considered the true and good, he was himself particularly attached. There is much, however, that speaks to the many. When he would consent to dismiss these huntings after the obscure (which, entwined with his nature as they were, he did with difficulty), no poet ever expressed in sweeter, more heart-reaching, or more passionate verse, the gentler or more forcible emotions of the soul.

Preface

A wise friend once wrote to Shelley: "You are still very young, and in certain essential respects you do not yet sufficiently perceive that you are so." It is seldom that the young know what youth is, till they have got beyond its period; and time was not given him to attain this knowledge. It must be remembered that there is the stamp of such inexperience on all he wrote; he had not completed his nine and twentieth year when he died. The calm of middle life did not add the seal of the virtues which adorn maturity to those generated by the vehement spirit of youth. Through life also he was a martyr to ill health, and constant pain wound up his nerves to a pitch of susceptibility that rendered his views of life different from those of a man in the enjoyment of healthy sensations. Perfectly gentle and forbearing in manner, he suffered a good deal of internal irritability, or rather excitement, and his fortitude to bear was almost always on the stretch; and thus, during a short life, had gone through more experience of sensation than many whose existence is protracted. "If I die to-morrow," he said, on the eve of his unanticipated death, "I have lived to be older than my father." The weight of thought and feeling burdened him heavily; you read his sufferings in his attenuated frame, while you perceived the mastery he held over them in his animated countenance and brilliant eyes.

He died, and the world showed no outward sign. But his influence over mankind, though slow in growth, is fast augmenting; and, in the ameliorations that have taken place in the political state of his country, we may trace in part the operation of his arduous struggles. His spirit gathers peace in its new state from the sense that, though late, his exertions were not made in vain, and in the progress of the liberty he so fondly loved.

He died, and his place, among those who knew him intimately, has never been filled up. He walked beside them like a spirit of good to comfort and benefit — to enlighten the darkness of life with irradiations of genius, to cheer it with his sympathy and love. Any one, once attached to Shelley, must feel all other affections, however true and fond, as wasted on barren soil in comparison. It is our best consolation to know that such a pure-minded and exalted being was once among us, and now

Preface

exists where we hope one day to join him; — although the intolerant, in their blindness, poured down anathemas, the Spirit of Good, who can judge the heart, never rejected him.

In the notes appended to the poems I have endeavoured to narrate the origin and history of each. The loss of nearly all letters and papers which refer to his early life renders the execution more imperfect than it would otherwise have been. I have, however, the liveliest recollection of all that was done and said during the period of my knowing him. Every impression is as clear as if stamped yesterday, and I have no apprehension of any mistake in my statements as far as they go. In other respects I am indeed incompetent: but I feel the importance of the task, and regard it as my most sacred duty. I endeavour to fulfil it in a manner he would himself approve; and hope, in this publication, to lay the first stone of a monument due to Shelley's genius, his sufferings, and his virtues:

Se al seguir son tarda,
Forse avverrà che 'l bel nome gentile
Consacrerò con questa stanca penna.

Postscript

In Second Edition of 1839

I N revising this new edition, and carefully consulting Shelley's scattered and confused papers, I found a few fragments which had hitherto escaped me, and was enabled to complete a few poems hitherto left unfinished. What at one time escapes the searching eye, dimmed by its own earnestness, becomes clear at a future period. By the aid of a friend, I also present some poems complete and correct which hitherto have been defaced by various mistakes and omissions. It was suggested that the poem " To the Queen of My Heart " was falsely attributed to Shelley. I certainly find no trace of it among his papers ; and, as those

Postscript

of his intimate friends whom I have consulted never heard of it, I omit it.

Two poems are added of some length, "Swellfoot the Tyrant" and "Peter Bell the Third." I have mentioned the circumstances under which they were written in the notes; and need only add that they are conceived in a very different spirit from Shelley's usual compositions. They are specimens of the burlesque and fanciful; but, although they adopt a familiar style and homely imagery, there shine through the radiance of the poet's imagination the earnest views and opinions of the politician and the moralist.

At my request the publisher has restored the omitted passages of " Queen Mab." I now present this edition as a complete collection of my husband's poetical works, and I do not foresee that I can hereafter add to or take away a word or line.

PUTNEY, *November 6, 1839.*

Preface by Mrs. Shelley

To the Volume of Posthumous Poems

Published in 1824

In nobil sangue vita umile e queta,
Ed in alto intelletto un puro core;
Frutto senile in sul giovenil fiore,
E in aspetto pensoso anima lieta.

PETRARCA.

T had been my wish, on presenting the public with the Posthumous Poems of Mr. Shelley, to have accompanied them by a biographical notice; as it appeared to me that at this moment a narration of the events of my husband's life would come more gracefully from other hands than mine, I applied to Mr. Leigh Hunt. The distinguished friendship that Mr. Shelley felt for him, and the enthusiastic affection with which Mr. Leigh Hunt clings to his friend's memory, seemed to point him out as

the person best calculated for such an under-taking. His absence from this country, which prevented our mutual explanation, has unfortu-nately rendered my scheme abortive. I do not doubt but that on some other occasion he will pay this tribute to his lost friend, and sincerely regret that the volume which I edit has not been honoured by its insertion.

The comparative solitude in which Mr. Shelley lived was the occasion that he was personally known to few; and his fearless enthusiasm in the cause which he considered the most sacred upon earth, the improvement of the moral and physical state of mankind, was the chief reason why he, like other illus-trious reformers, was pursued by hatred and calumny. No man was ever more devoted than he to the endeavour of making those around him happy; no man ever possessed friends more unfeignedly attached to him. The ungrateful world did not feel his loss, and the gap it made seemed to close as quickly over his memory as the murderous sea above his living frame. Hereafter men will lament that his transcendent powers of intellect were extinguished before they had bestowed on them their choicest treasures. To his friends his loss is irremediable : the wise, the brave, the gentle, is gone for ever ! He is to them as a bright vision, whose radiant track, left behind in the memory, is worth all the realities that society can afford. Before the critics contradict me, let them appeal to any one who had ever known him. To see him was to love him : and his presence, like Ithuriel's spear, was alone sufficient to disclose the falsehood of the tale which his enemies whispered in the ear of the ignorant world.

His life was spent in the contemplation of Nature, in arduous study, or in acts of kindness and affection. He was an elegant scholar and a profound metaphysician ; without possessing much scientific knowledge, he was unrivalled in the justness and extent of his observations on natural objects ; he knew every plant by its name, and was familiar with the history and habits of every production of the earth ; he could interpret without a fault each appearance in the sky ; and the varied phenomena of heaven and earth filled him with deep emotion. He made his study and reading-room of the shadowed copse, the stream, the

Preface

lake, and the waterfall. Ill health and continual pain preyed upon his powers; and the solitude in which we lived, particularly on our first arrival in Italy, although congenial to his feelings, must frequently have weighed upon his spirits; those beautiful and affecting " Lines Written in Dejection near Naples " were composed at such an interval; but, when in health, his spirits were buoyant and youthful to an extraordinary degree.

Such was his love for Nature that every page of his poetry is associated, in the minds of his friends, with the loveliest scenes of the countries which he inhabited. In early life he visited the most beautiful parts of this country and Ireland. Afterward the Alps of Switzerland became his inspirers. " Prometheus Unbound " was written among the deserted and flower-grown ruins of Rome; and, when he made his home under the Pisan hills, their roofless recesses harboured him as he composed the " Witch of Atlas," " Adonais," and " Hellas." In the wild but beautiful Bay of Spezzia, the winds and waves which he loved became his playmates. His days were chiefly spent on the water; the management of his boat, its alterations and improvements, were his principal occupation. At night, when the unclouded moon shone on the calm sea, he often went alone in his little shallop to the rocky caves that bordered it, and, sitting beneath their shelter, wrote the " Triumph of Life," the last of his productions. The beauty but strangeness of this lonely place, the refined pleasure which he felt in the companionship of a few selected friends, our entire sequestration from the rest of the world, all contributed to render this period of his life one of continued enjoyment. I am convinced that the two months we passed there were the happiest which he had ever known: his health even rapidly improved, and he was never better than when I last saw him, full of spirits and joy, embark for Leghorn, that he might there welcome Leigh Hunt to Italy. I was to have accompanied him; but illness confined me to my room, and thus put the seal on my misfortune. His vessel bore out of sight with a favourable wind, and I remained awaiting his return by the breakers of that sea which was about to engulf him.

He spent a week at Pisa, employed in kind

offices toward his friend, and enjoying with keen delight the renewal of their intercourse. He then embarked with Mr. Williams, the chosen and beloved sharer of his pleasures and of his fate, to return to us. We waited for them in vain; the sea by its restless moaning seemed to desire to inform us of what we would not learn, — but a veil may well be drawn over such misery. The real anguish of those moments transcended all the fictions that the most glowing imagination ever portrayed; our seclusion, the savage nature of the inhabitants of the surrounding villages, and our immediate vicinity to the troubled sea, combined to imbue with strange horror our days of uncertainty. The truth was at last known, — a truth that made our loved and lovely Italy appear a tomb, its sky a pall. Every heart echoed the deep lament, and my only consolation was in the praise and earnest love that each voice bestowed and each countenance demonstrated for him we had lost, — not, I fondly hope, for ever; his unearthly and elevated nature is a pledge of the continuation of his being, although in an altered form. Rome received his ashes; they are deposited beneath its weed-grown wall, and " the world's sole monument " is enriched by his remains.

I must add a few words concerning the contents of this volume. " Julian and Maddalo," the " Witch of Atlas," and most of the translations, were written some years ago ; and, with the exception of the " Cyclops," and the scenes from the " Magico Prodigioso," may be considered as having received the author's ultimate corrections. The " Triumph of Life " was his last work, and was left in so unfinished a state that I arranged it in its present form with great difficulty. All his poems which were scattered in periodical works are collected in this volume, and I have added a reprint of " Alastor, or the Spirit of Solitude : " the difficulty with which a copy can be obtained is the cause of its republication. Many of the miscellaneous poems, written on the spur of the occasion, and never retouched, I found among his manuscript books, and have carefully copied. I have subjoined, whenever I have been able, the date of their composition.

I do not know whether the critics will reprehend the insertion of some of the most imperfect among them ; but I frankly own that I have been more actuated by the fear lest any monument of his genius should escape me than the wish of presenting nothing but what was complete to the fastidious reader. I feel secure that the lovers of Shelley's poetry (who know how, more than any poet of the present day, every line and word he wrote is instinct with peculiar beauty) will pardon and thank me: I consecrate this volume to them.

The size of this collection has prevented the insertion of any prose pieces. They will hereafter appear in a separate publication.

MARY W. SHELLEY.

LONDON, *June 1, 1824.*

Queen Mab

A Philosophical Poem with Notes

Ecrasez l'infame !
Correspondance de Voltaire.

Avia Pieridum peragro loca, nullius ante
Trita solo ; juvat integros accedere fonteis ;
Atque haurire : juvatque novos decerpere flores.

.   .   .   .

Unde prius nulli velarint tempora musæ.
Primum quod magnis doceo de rebus ; et arctis
Religionum animos nodis exsolvere pergo.
Lucret. lib. iv.

Δος του στῶ, χαὶ χοσμον χινησω.
Archimedes.

To Harriet ——

WHOSE is the love that gleaming
        through the world,
    Wards off the poisonous arrow of
        its scorn?
  Whose is the warm and partial praise,
  Virtue's most sweet reward?

Beneath whose looks did my reviving soul
Riper in truth and virtuous daring grow?
  Whose eyes have I gazed fondly on;
  And loved mankind the more?

Harriet! on thine:—thou wert my purer
    mind;
Thou wert the inspiration of my song;
  Thine are these early wilding flowers,
  Though garlanded by me.

Dedication

Then press into thy breast this pledge of love;
And know, though time may change and years
    may roll,
  Each floweret gathered in my heart
  It consecrates to thine.

Queen Mab

I.

HOW wonderful is Death,
　　Death and his brother Sleep !
　　One, pale as yonder waning moon
　　　With lips of lurid blue;
The other, rosy as the morn
　　When throned on ocean's wave
　　It blushes o'er the world :
Yet both so passing wonderful !

　　Hath then the gloomy Power
Whose reign is in the tainted sepulchres
　　Seized on her sinless soul ?
　　Must then that peerless form
Which love and admiration cannot view
Without a beating heart, those azure veins

Queen Mab

Which steal like streams along a field of snow,
  That lovely outline, which is fair
    As breathing marble, perish?
    Must putrefaction's breath
  Leave nothing of this heavenly sight
    But loathsomeness and ruin?
Spare nothing but a gloomy theme,
On which the lightest heart might moralize?
  Or is it only a sweet slumber
    Stealing o'er sensation,
  Which the breath of roseate morning
    Chaseth into darkness?
    Will Ianthe wake again,
And give that faithful bosom joy
Whose sleepless spirit waits to catch
Light, life and rapture from her smile?

    Yes! she will wake again,
Although her glowing limbs are motionless,
    And silent those sweet lips,
    Once breathing eloquence,
  That might have soothed a tiger's rage,
Or thawed the cold heart of a conqueror.

Queen Mab

Her dewy eyes are closed,
And on their lids, whose texture fine
Scarce hides the dark blue orbs beneath,
    The baby Sleep is pillowed:
    Her golden tresses shade
    The bosom's stainless pride,
Curling like tendrils of the parasite
    Around a marble column.

    Hark! whence that rushing sound?
    'Tis like the wondrous strain
That round a lonely ruin swells,
Which, wandering on the echoing shore,
    The enthusiast hears at evening:
    'Tis softer than the west wind's sigh;
    'Tis wilder than the unmeasured notes
Of that strange lyre whose strings
The genii of the breezes sweep:
    Those lines of rainbow light
Are like the moonbeams when they fall
Through some cathedral window, but the teints
    Are such as may not find
    Comparison on earth.

Queen Mab

Behold the chariot of the Fairy Queen!
Celestial coursers paw the unyielding air;
Their filmy pennons at her word they furl,
And stop obedient to the reins of light:
    These the Queen of spells drew in,
    She spread a charm around the spot,
And leaning graceful from the ethereal car,
    Long did she gaze, and silently,
        Upon the slumbering maid.

Oh! not the visioned poet in his dreams,
When   silvery   clouds   float   through   the
    wildered brain,
When every sight of lovely, wild and grand
    Astonishes, enraptures, elevates,
        When fancy at a glance combines
        The wondrous and the beautiful, —
    So bright, so fair, so wild a shape
        Hath ever yet beheld,
As that which reined the coursers of the
    air,
    And poured the magic of her gaze
        Upon the maiden's sleep.

8

Queen Mab

The broad and yellow moon
Shone dimly through her form —
That form of faultless symmetry;
The pearly and pellucid car
Moved not the moonlight's line:
'Twas not an earthly pageant:
Those who had looked upon the sight,
Passing all human glory,
Saw not the yellow moon,
Saw not the mortal scene,
Heard not the night-wind's rush,
Heard not an earthly sound,
Saw but the fairy pageant,
Heard but the heavenly strains
That filled the lonely dwelling.

The Fairy's frame was slight, yon fibrous
cloud,
That catches but the palest tinge of even,
And which the straining eye can hardly seize
When melting into eastern twilight's shadow,
Were scarce so thin, so slight; but the fair
star

Queen Mab

That gems the glittering coronet of morn,
Sheds not a light so mild, so powerful,
As that which, bursting from the Fairy's
    form,
Spread a purpureal halo round the scene,
  Yet with an undulating motion,
  Swayed to her outline gracefully.

    From her celestial car
    The Fairy Queen descended,
    And thrice she waved her wand
Circled with wreaths of amaranth:
    Her thin and misty form
    Moved with the moving air,
    And the clear silver tones,
    As thus she spoke, were such
As are unheard by all but gifted ear.

FAIRY

Stars! your balmiest influence shed!
Elements! your wrath suspend!
Sleep, Ocean, in the rocky bounds
    That circle thy domain!

Queen Mab

Let not a breath be seen to stir
Around yon grass-grown ruin's height,
   Let even the restless gossamer
      Sleep on the moveless air!
      Soul of Ianthe! thou,
Judged alone worthy of the envied boon,
That waits the good and the sincere; that
   waits
Those who have struggled, and with resolute
   will
Vanquished earth's pride and meanness, burst
   the chains,
The icy chains of custom, and have shone
The day-stars of their age; — Soul of
   Ianthe!
      Awake! arise!

      Sudden arose
      Ianthe's Soul; it stood
All beautiful in naked purity,
The perfect semblance of its bodily frame.
Instinct with inexpressible beauty and grace,
      Each stain of earthliness

Queen Mab

Had passed away, it reassumed
Its native dignity, and stood
    Immortal amid ruin.

    Upon the couch the body lay
    Wrapt in the depth of slumber:
Its features were fixed and meaningless,
    Yet animal life was there,
And every organ yet performed
Its natural functions: 'twas a sight
Of wonder to behold the body and soul.
    The selfsame lineaments, the same
    Marks of identity were there:
Yet, oh, how different!   One aspires to
    Heaven,
Pants for its sempiternal heritage,
And ever-changing, ever-rising still,
    Wantons in endless being.
The other, for a time the unwilling sport
Of circumstance and passion, struggles on;
Fleets through its sad duration rapidly:
Then like an useless and worn-out machine,
    Rots, perishes, and passes.

Queen Mab

FAIRY

Spirit! who hast dived so deep;
Spirit! who hast soared so high;
Thou the fearless, thou the mild,
Accept the boon thy worth hath earned,
Ascend the car with me.

SPIRIT

Do I dream?   Is this new feeling
But a visioned ghost of slumber?
If indeed I am a soul,
A free, a disembodied soul,
Speak again to me.

FAIRY

I am the Fairy MAB: to me 'tis given
The wonders of the human world to keep:
The secrets of the immeasurable past,
In the unfailing consciences of men,
Those stern, unflattering chronicles, I find:
The future, from the causes which arise
In each event, I gather: not the sting
Which retributive memory implants

Queen Mab

In the hard bosom of the selfish man;
Nor that ecstatic and exulting throb
Which virtue's votary feels when he sums up
The thoughts and actions of a well-spent day
Are unforeseen, unregistered by me:
And it is yet permitted me, to rend
The veil of mortal frailty, that the spirit,
Clothed in its changeless purity, may know
How soonest to accomplish the great end
For which it hath its being, and may taste
That peace, which in the end all life will share.
This is the meed of virtue; happy Soul,
    Ascend the car with me!

  The chains of earth's immurement
    Fell from Ianthe's spirit;
They shrank and brake like bandages of straw
  Beneath a wakened giant's strength.
    She knew her glorious change,
  And felt in apprehension uncontrolled
    New raptures opening round:
Each day-dream of her mortal life,
Each frenzied vision of the slumbers

Queen Mab

That closed each well-spent day,
Seemed now to meet reality.
The Fairy and the Soul proceeded;
The silver clouds disparted;
And as the car of magic they ascended,
Again the speechless music swelled,
Again the coursers of the air
Unfurled their azure pennons, and the Queen
Shaking the beamy reins
Bade them pursue their way.

The magic car moved on.
The night was fair, and countless stars
Studded heaven's dark blue vault, —
Just o'er the eastern wave
Peeped the first faint smile of morn: —
The magic car moved on —
From the celestial hoofs
The atmosphere in flaming sparkles flew,
And where the burning wheels
Eddied above the mountain's loftiest peak,
Was traced a line of lightning.
Now it flew far above a rock,

Queen Mab

The utmost verge of earth,
The rival of the Andes, whose dark brow
Lowered o'er the silver sea.

Far, far below the chariot's path,
   Calm as a slumbering babe,
   Tremendous Ocean lay.
The mirror of its stillness showed
   The pale and waning stars,
   The chariot's fiery track,
   And the gray light of morn
   Tingeing those fleecy clouds
   That canopied the dawn.
Seemed it, that the chariot's way
Lay through the midst of an immense concave,
Radiant with million constellations, tinged
   With shades of infinite colour,
   And semicircled with a belt
   Flashing incessant meteors.

   The magic car moved on.
   As they approached their goal

Queen Mab

The coursers seemed to gather speed;
The sea no longer was distinguished; earth
Appeared a vast and shadowy sphere;
    The sun's unclouded orb
    Rolled through the black concave;
    Its rays of rapid light
Parted around the chariot's swifter course,
  And fell, like ocean's feathery spray
    Dashed from the boiling surge
    Before a vessel's prow.

    The magic car moved on.
    Earth's distant orb appeared
The smallest light that twinkles in the heaven;
    Whilst round the chariot's way
    Innumerable systems rolled,
    And countless spheres diffused
    An ever-varying glory.
  It was a sight of wonder: some
  Were hornèd like the crescent moon;
  Some shed a mild and silver beam
  Like Hesperus o'er the western sea;
  Some dash'd athwart with trains of flame,

17

Queen Mab

Like worlds to death and ruin driven ;
Some shone like suns, and, as the chariot
    passed,
        Eclipsed all other light.

        Spirit of Nature ! here !
In this interminable wilderness
Of worlds, at whose immensity
    Even soaring fancy staggers,
    Here is thy fitting temple.
        Yet not the lightest leaf
That quivers to the passing breeze
        Is less instinct with thee :
        Yet not the meanest worm
That lurks in graves and fattens on the dead
    Less shares thy eternal breath.
        Spirit of Nature ! thou !
Imperishable as this scene,
        Here is thy fitting temple.

II.

IF solitude hath ever led thy steps
    To the wild ocean's echoing shore,
      And thou hast lingered there,
      Until the sun's broad orb
Seemed resting on the burnished wave,
    Thou must have marked the lines
Of purple gold, that motionless
      Hung o'er the sinking sphere:
Thou must have marked the billowy clouds
Edged with intolerable radiancy
      Towering like rocks of jet
      Crowned with a diamond wreath.
      And yet there is a moment,
      When the sun's highest point
Peeps like a star o'er ocean's western edge,
When those far clouds of feathery gold,
    Shaded with deepest purple, gleam
    Like islands on a dark blue sea;

Queen Mab

Then has thy fancy soared above the earth,
    And furled its wearied wing
    Within the Fairy's fane.

        Yet not the golden islands
        Gleaming in yon flood of light,
            Nor the feathery curtains
        Stretching o'er the sun's bright couch,
        Nor the burnished ocean waves
            Paving that gorgeous dome,
    So fair, so wonderful a sight
As Mab's ethereal palace could afford.
Yet likest evening's vault, that faery Hall!
As Heaven, low resting on the wave, it
    spread
        Its floors of flashing light,
        Its vast and azure dome,
        Its fertile golden islands
        Floating on a silver sea;
Whilst suns their mingling beamings darted
Through clouds of circumambient darkness,
    And pearly battlements around
    Looked o'er the immense of Heaven.

Queen Mab

The magic car no longer moved.
    The Fairy and the Spirit
    Entered the Hall of Spells:
    Those golden clouds
That rolled in glittering billows
Beneath the azure canopy
With the ethereal footsteps trembled not
    The light and crimson mists,
Floating to strains of thrilling melody
    Through that unearthly dwelling,
Yielded to every movement of the will.
Upon their passive swell the Spirit leaned,
And, for the varied bliss that pressed around,
    Used not the glorious privilege
    Of virtue and of wisdom.

    Spirit! the Fairy said,
And pointed to the gorgeous dome,
    This is a wondrous sight
    And mocks all human grandeur;
But, were it virtue's only meed to dwell
In a celestial palace, all resigned
To pleasurable impulses, immured

Queen Mab

Within the prison of itself, the will
Of changeless nature would be unfulfilled.
Learn to make others happy.   Spirit, come !
This is thine high reward : — the past shall rise ;
Thou shalt behold the present ; I will teach
        The secrets of the future.

        The Fairy and the Spirit
Approached the overhanging battlement. —
        Below lay stretched the universe !
        There, far as the remotest line
        That bounds imagination's flight,
            Countless and unending orbs
        In mazy motion intermingled,
        Yet still fulfilled immutably
                Eternal nature's law.
                Above, below, around
                The circling systems formed
        A wilderness of harmony ;
        Each with undeviating aim,
In eloquent silence, through the depths of
    space
                Pursued its wondrous way.

Queen Mab

There was a little light
That twinkled in the misty distance :
    None but a spirit's eye
    Might ken that rolling orb ;
    None but a spirit's eye,
    And in no other place
But that celestial dwelling, might behold
Each action of this earth's inhabitants.
    But matter, space and time
In those aerial mansions cease to act ;
And all-prevailing wisdom, when it reaps
The harvest of its excellence, o'erbounds
Those obstacles, of which an earthly soul
    Fears to attempt the conquest.

    The Fairy pointed to the earth.
    The Spirit's intellectual eye
    Its kindred beings recognized.
The thronging thousands, to a passing
    view,
    Seemed like an ant-hill's citizens.
    How wonderful ! that even
The passions, prejudices, interests,

Queen Mab

That sway the meanest being, the weak touch
    That moves the finest nerve,
    And in one human brain
Causes the faintest thought, becomes a link
    In the great chain of nature.

    Behold, the Fairy cried,
Palmyra's ruined palaces ! —
    Behold ! where grandeur frowned ;
    Behold ! where pleasure smiled ;
What now remains ? — the memory
    Of senselessness and shame —
    What is immortal there?
    Nothing — it stands to tell
    A melancholy tale, to give
    An awful warning : soon
Oblivion will steal silently
    The remnant of its fame.
    Monarchs and conquerors there
Proud o'er prostrate millions trod —
The earthquakes of the human race ;
Like them, forgotten when the ruin
    That marks their shock is past.

Queen Mab

Beside the eternal Nile,
    The Pyramids have risen.
Nile shall pursue his changeless way:
    Those pyramids shall fall;
Yea! not a stone shall stand to tell
    The spot whereon they stood!
Their very site shall be forgotten,
    As is their builder's name!

    Behold yon sterile spot;
Where now the wandering Arab's tent
    Flaps in the desert-blast.
There once old Salem's haughty fane
Reared high to heaven its thousand golden
    domes,
    And in the blushing face of day
    Exposed its shameful glory.
Oh! many a widow, many an orphan cursed
The building of that fane; and many a father,
Worn out with toil and slavery, implored
The poor man's God to sweep it from the
    earth,
And spare his children the detested task

Of piling stone on stone, and poisoning
 The choicest days of life,
 To soothe a dotard's vanity.
There an inhuman and uncultured race
Howled hideous praises to their Demon-God;
They rushed to war, tore from the mother's
 womb
The unborn child, — old age and infancy
Promiscuous perished; their victorious arms
Left not a soul to breathe. Oh! they were
 fiends:
But what was he who taught them that the
 God
Of nature and benevolence hath given
A special sanction to the trade of blood?
His name and theirs are fading, and the tales
Of this barbarian nation, which imposture
Recites till terror credits, are pursuing
 Itself into forgetfulness.
 Where Athens, Rome, and Sparta stood,
 There is a moral desert now:
 The mean and miserable huts,
 The yet more wretched palaces,

Queen Mab

Contrasted with those ancient fanes
Now crumbling to oblivion;
The long and lonely colonnades,
Through which the ghost of Freedom stalks,
    Seem like a well-known tune,
Which, in some dear scene we have loved to
    hear,
      Remembered now in sadness.
      But, oh ! how much more changed,
      How gloomier is the contrast
      Of human nature there !
Where Socrates expired, a tyrant's slave,
A coward and a fool, spreads death around —
    Then, shuddering, meets his own.
Where Cicero and Antoninus lived,
    A cowled and hypocritical monk
      Prays, curses and deceives.

      Spirit ! ten thousand years
      Have scarcely passed away,
Since, in the waste where now the savage
    drinks
His enemy's blood, and aping Europe's sons,

Queen Mab

Wakes the unholy song of war,
　Arose a stately city,
Metropolis of the western continent:
　There, now, the mossy column-stone,
Indented by time's unrelaxing grasp,
　　Which once appeared to brave
　　All, save its country's ruin;
　　There the wide forest scene,
Rude in the uncultivated loveliness
　　Of gardens long run wild,
Seems, to the unwilling sojourner, whose steps
　Chance in that desert has delayed,
Thus to have stood since earth was what it is.
　Yet once it was the busiest haunt,
Whither, as to a common centre, flocked
　Strangers and ships, and merchandise:
　　Once peace and freedom blest
　　The cultivated plain:
　　But wealth, that curse of man,
Blighted the bud of its prosperity:
Virtue and wisdom, truth and liberty,
Fled, to return not, until man shall know
　That they alone can give the bliss

Queen Mab

Worthy a soul that claims
Its kindred with eternity.

There's not one atom of yon earth
But once was living man;
Nor the minutest drop of rain,
That hangeth in its thinnest cloud,
But flowed in human veins:
And from the burning plains
Where Libyan monsters yell,
From the most gloomy glens
Of Greenland's sunless clime,
To where the golden fields
Of fertile England spread
Their harvest to the day,
Thou canst not find one spot
Whereon no city stood.

How strange is human pride!
I tell thee that those living things,
To whom the fragile blade of grass,
That springeth in the morn
And perisheth ere noon

Queen Mab

Is an unbounded world;
I tell thee that those viewless beings,
Whose mansion is the smallest particle
 Of the impassive atmosphere,
  Think, feel and live like man;
That their affections and antipathies,
  Like his, produce the laws
  Ruling their moral state;
  And the minutest throb
That through their frame diffuses
  The slightest, faintest motion,
  Is fixed and indispensable
  As the majestic laws
  That rule yon rolling orbs.

The Fairy paused. The Spirit,
In ecstasy of admiration, felt
All knowledge of the past revived; the events
  Of old and wondrous times,
Which dim tradition interruptedly
Teaches the credulous vulgar, were unfolded
 In just perspective to the view;
 Yet dim from their infinitude.

Queen Mab

The Spirit seemed to stand
High on an isolated pinnacle;
The flood of ages combating below,
The depth of the unbounded universe
Above, and all around
Nature's unchanging harmony.

III.

FAIRY! the Spirit said,
　　And on the Queen of spells
　　Fixed her ethereal eyes,
　　I thank thee.　Thou hast given
A boon which I will not resign, and taught
A lesson not to be unlearned.　I know
The past, and thence I will essay to glean
A warning for the future, so that man
May profit by his errors, and derive
　　Experience from his folly:
For, when the power of imparting joy
Is equal to the will, the human soul
　　Requires no other heaven.

MAB

Turn thee, surpassing Spirit!
Much yet remains unscanned.

Queen Mab

Thou knowest how great is man,
Thou knowest his imbecility :
    Yet learn thou what he is ;
    Yet learn the lofty destiny
    Which restless time prepares
    For every living soul.

Behold a gorgeous palace, that, amid
Yon populous city, rears its thousand towers
And seems itself a city.   Gloomy troops
Of sentinels, in stern and silent ranks,
Encompass it around : the dweller there
Cannot be free and happy ; hearest thou not
The curses of the fatherless, the groans
Of those who have no friend ?   He passes on :
The King, the wearer of a gilded chain
That binds his soul to abjectness, the fool
Whom courtiers nickname monarch, whilst a
    slave
Even to the basest appetites — that man
Heeds not the shriek of penury ; he smiles
At the deep curses which the destitute
Mutter in secret, and a sullen joy

Pervades his bloodless heart when thousands
    groan
But for those morsels which his wantonness
Wastes in unjoyous revelry, to save
All that they love from famine: when he
    hears
The tale of horror, to some ready-made face
Of hypocritical assent he turns,
Smothering the glow of shame, that, spite of
    him,
Flushes his bloated cheek.
                  Now to the meal
Of silence, grandeur, and excess, he drags
His palled unwilling appetite. If gold,
Gleaming around, and numerous viands culled
From every clime, could force the loathing
    sense
To overcome satiety, — if wealth
The spring it draws from poisons not, — or
    vice,
Unfeeling, stubborn vice, converteth not
Its food to deadliest venom; then that king
Is happy; and the peasant who fulfils

His unforced task, when he returns at even,
And by the blazing faggot meets again
Her welcome for whom all his toil is sped,
Tastes not a sweeter meal.

       Behold him now
Stretched on the gorgeous couch; his fevered
   brain
Reels dizzily awhile: but ah! too soon
The slumber of intemperance subsides,
And conscience, that undying serpent, calls
Her venomous brood to their nocturnal task.
Listen! he speaks! oh! mark that frenzied
   eye —
Oh! mark that deadly visage.

KING

       No cessation!
Oh! must this last for ever! Awful death,
I wish, yet fear to clasp thee! Not one mo-
   ment
Of dreamless sleep! O dear and blessèd
   peace!
Why dost thou shroud thy vestal purity

Queen Mab

In penury and dungeons? wherefore lurkest
With danger, death, and solitude; yet shun'st
The palace I have built thee?   Sacred peace!
Oh visit me but once, but pitying shed
One drop of balm upon my withered soul.

Vain man! that palace is the virtuous heart,
And peace defileth not her snowy robes
In such a shed as thine.   Hark! yet he mut-
    ters;
His slumbers are but varied agonies,
They prey like scorpions on the springs of life.
There needeth not the hell that bigots frame
To punish those who err: earth in itself
Contains at once the evil and the cure;
And all-sufficing nature can chastise
Those who transgress her law, — she only
    knows
How justly to proportion to the fault
The punishment it merits.
                          Is it strange
That this poor wretch should pride him in his
    woe?

Queen Mab

Take pleasure in its abjectness, and hug

The scorpion that consumes him? Is it strange

That, placed on a conspicuous throne of thorns,

Grasping an iron sceptre, and immured

Within a splendid prison, whose stern bounds

Shut him from all that's good or dear on earth,

His soul asserts not its humanity?

That man's mild nature rises not in war

Against a king's employ? No — 'tis not strange.

He, like the vulgar, thinks, feels, acts and lives

Just as his father did; the unconquered powers

Of precedent and custom interpose

Between a *king* and virtue. Stranger yet,

To those who know not nature, nor deduce

The future from the present, it may seem,

That not one slave, who suffers from the crimes

Of this unnatural being; not one wretch,

Queen Mab

Whose children famish, and whose nuptial bed
Is earth's unpitying bosom, rears an arm
To dash him from his throne!

                              Those gilded flies
That, basking in the sunshine of a court,
Fatten on its corruption!—what are they?
—The drones of the community; they feed
On the mechanic's labour: the starved hind
For them compels the stubborn glebe to yield
Its unshared harvests; and yon squalid form,
Leaner than fleshless misery, that wastes
A sunless life in the unwholesome mine,
Drags out in labour a protracted death,
To glut their grandeur; many faint with toil,
That few may know the cares and woe of
    sloth.

Whence, think'st thou, kings and parasites
    arose?
Whence that unnatural line of drones, who
    heap
Toil and unvanquishable penury
On those who build their palaces, and bring

Queen Mab

Their daily bread ? — From vice, black loath-
    some vice;
From rapine, madness, treachery, and wrong;
From all that genders misery, and makes
Of earth this thorny wilderness; from lust,
Revenge, and murder. . . . And when rea-
    son's voice,
Loud as the voice of nature, shall have waked
The nations; and mankind perceive that vice
Is discord, war, and misery; that virtue
Is peace, and happiness and harmony;
When man's maturer nature shall disdain
The playthings of its childhood; — kingly glare
Will lose its power to dazzle; its authority
Will silently pass by; the gorgeous throne
Shall stand unnoticed in the regal hall,
Fast falling to decay; whilst falsehood's trade
Shall be as hateful and unprofitable
As that of truth is now.
               Where is the fame
Which the vainglorious mighty of the earth
Seek to eternize? Oh! the faintest sound
From time's light footfall, the minutest wave

Queen Mab

That swells the flood of ages, whelms in
    nothing
The unsubstantial bubble. Aye! to-day
Stern is the tyrant's mandate, red the gaze
That flashes desolation, strong the arm
That scatters multitudes. To-morrow comes!
That mandate is a thunder-peal that died
In ages past; that gaze, a transient flash
On which the midnight closed, and on that arm
The worm has made his meal.
                  The virtuous man,
Who, great in his humility, as kings
Are little in their grandeur; he who leads
Invincibly a life of resolute good,
And stands amid the silent dungeon-depths
More free and fearless than the trembling
    judge,
Who, clothed in venal power, vainly strove
To bind the impassive spirit; — when he falls,
His mild eye beams benevolence no more:
Withered the hand outstretched but to relieve;
Sunk reason's simple eloquence, that rolled
But to appal the guilty. Yes! the grave

Queen Mab

Hath quenched that eye, and death's relentless
    frost
Withered that arm : but the unfading fame
Which virtue hangs upon its votary's tomb ;
The deathless memory of that man, whom kings
Call to their mind and tremble ; the remem-
    brance
With which the happy spirit contemplates
Its well-spent pilgrimage on earth,
Shall never pass away.

Nature rejects the monarch, not the man ;
The subject, not the citizen : for kings
And subjects, mutual foes, for ever play
A losing game into each other's hands,
Whose stakes are vice and misery.   The man
Of virtuous soul commands not, nor obeys.
Power, like a desolating pestilence,
Pollutes whate'er it touches ; and obedience,
Bane of all genius, virtue, freedom, truth,
Makes slaves of men, and, of the human
    frame,
A mechanized automaton.

Queen Mab

> When Nero,
> High over flaming Rome, with savage joy
> Lowered like a fiend, drank with enraptured
>   ear
> The shrieks of agonizing death, beheld
> The frightful desolation spread, and felt
> A new created sense within his soul
> Thrill to the sight, and vibrate to the sound;
> Think'st thou his grandeur had not overcome
> The force of human kindness? and, when
>   Rome,
> With one stern blow, hurled not the tyrant
>   down,
> Crushed not the arm red with her dearest
>   blood,
> Had not submissive abjectness destroyed
> Nature's suggestions?
>   Look on yonder earth:
> The golden harvests spring; the unfailing sun
> Sheds light and life; the fruits, the flowers,
>   the trees,
> Arise in due succession; all things speak
> Peace, harmony, and love.   The universe,

Queen Mab

In nature's silent eloquence, declares
That all fulfil the works of love and joy, —
All but the outcast man.   He fabricates
The sword which stabs his peace ; he cherisheth
The snakes that gnaw his heart; he raiseth
    up
The tyrant, whose delight is in his woe,
Whose sport is in his agony.   Yon sun,
Lights it the great alone?   Yon silver beams,
Sleep they less sweetly on the cottage thatch
Than on the dome of kings?   Is mother
    earth
A step-dame to her numerous sons, who earn
Her unshared gifts with unremitting toil ;
A mother only to those puling babes
Who, nursed in ease and luxury, make men
The playthings of their babyhood, and mar,
In self-important childishness, that peace
Which men alone appreciate?

     Spirit of Nature ! no.
The pure diffusion of thy essence throbs
  Alike in every human heart.

Queen Mab

Thou, aye, erectest there
Thy throne of power unappealable:
Thou art the judge beneath whose nod
Man's brief and frail authority
Is powerless as the wind
That passeth idly by.
Thine the tribunal which surpasseth
The show of human justice,
As God surpasses man.

Spirit of Nature! thou
Life of interminable multitudes;
Soul of those mighty spheres
Whose changeless paths thro' Heaven's deep
silence lie;
Soul of that smallest being,
The dwelling of whose life
Is one faint April sun-gleam; —
Man, like these passive things,
Thy will unconsciously fulfilleth:
Like theirs, his age of endless peace,
Which time is fast maturing,
Will swiftly, surely come;

And the unbounded frame, which thou per-
  vadest,
   Will be without a flaw
  Marring its perfect symmetry.

IV.

HOW beautiful this night! the balmiest sigh
    Which vernal zephyrs breathe in evening's ear,
Were discord to the speaking quietude
That wraps this moveless scene. Heaven's ebon vault,
Studded with stars unutterably bright,
Through which the moon's unclouded grandeur rolls,
Seems like a canopy which love had spread
To curtain her sleeping world. Yon gentle hills,
Robed in a garment of untrodden snow;
Yon darksome rocks, whence icicles depend,
So stainless, that their white and glittering spires

46

Queen Mab

Tinge not the moon's pure beam; yon castled
    steep,
Whose banner hangeth o'er the time-worn
    tower
So idly, that rapt fancy deemeth it
A metaphor of peace; — all form a scene
Where musing solitude might love to lift
Her soul above this sphere of earthliness;
Where silence undisturbed might watch alone,
So cold, so bright, so still.
                The orb of day,
In southern climes, o'er ocean's waveless field
Sinks sweetly smiling: not the faintest breath
Steals o'er the unruffled deep; the clouds of
    eve
Reflect unmoved the lingering beam of day;
And vesper's image on the western main
Is beautifully still. To-morrow comes:
Cloud upon cloud, in dark and deepening
    mass,
Roll o'er the blackened waters; the deep roar
Of distant thunder mutters awfully;
Tempest unfolds its pinion o'er the gloom

That shrouds the boiling surge; the pitiless
    fiend,
With all his winds and lightnings, tracks his
    prey;
The torn deep yawns,—the vessel finds a grave
Beneath its jaggèd gulph.

                  Ah! whence yon glare
That fires the arch of heaven?—that dark red
    smoke
Blotting the silver moon? The stars are
    quenched
In darkness, and the pure and spangling snow
Gleams faintly through the gloom that gathers
    round!
Hark to that roar, whose swift and deaf'ning
    peals
In countless echoes through the mountains
    ring,
Startling pale midnight on her starry throne!
Now swells the intermingling din; the jar
Frequent and frightful of the bursting bomb;
The falling beam, the shriek, the groan, the
    shout,

Queen Mab

The ceaseless clangour, and the rush of men
Inebriate with rage : — loud, and more loud
The discord grows ; till pale death shuts the
    scene,
And o'er the conqueror and the conquered
    draws
His cold and bloody shroud. — Of all the men
Whom day's departing beam saw blooming
    there,
In proud and vigorous health ; of all the hearts
That beat with anxious life at sunset there ;
How few survive, how few are beating now !
All is deep silence, like the fearful calm
That slumbers in the storm's portentous pause ;
Save when the frantic wail of widowed love
Comes shuddering on the blast, or the faint
    moan
With which some soul bursts from the frame
    of clay
Wrapt round its struggling powers.
                      The gray morn
Dawns on the mournful scene ; the sulphurous
    smoke

Queen Mab

Before the icy wind slow rolls away,
And the bright beams of frosty morning dance
Along the spangling snow. There tracks of
    blood
Even to the forest's depth, and scattered arms,
And lifeless warriors, whose hard lineaments
Death's self could change not, mark the dread-
    ful path
Of the outsallying victors : far behind,
Black ashes note where their proud city stood.
Within yon forest is a gloomy glen —
Each tree which guards its darkness from the
    day
Waves o'er a warrior's tomb.

                      I see thee shrink,
Surpassing Spirit ! — wert thou human else ?
I see a shade of doubt and horror fleet
Across thy stainless features : yet fear not ;
This is no unconnected misery,
Nor stands uncaused, and irretrievable.
Man's evil nature, that apology
Which kings who rule, and cowards who crouch,
    set up

Queen Mab

For their unnumbered crimes, sheds not the
    blood
Which desolates the discord-wasted land.
From kings, and priests, and statesmen, war
    arose,
Whose safety is man's deep unbettered woe,
Whose grandeur his debasement.   Let the axe
Strike at the root, the poison-tree will fall;
And where its venomed exhalations spread
Ruin, and death, and woe, where millions lay
Quenching the serpent's famine, and their bones
Bleaching unburied in the putrid blast,
A garden shall arise, in loveliness
Surpassing fabled Eden.

                    Hath Nature's soul,
That formed this world so beautiful, that spread
Earth's lap with plenty, and life's smallest chord
Strung to unchanging unison, that gave
The happy birds their dwelling in the grove,
That yielded to the wanderers of the deep
The lovely silence of the unfathomed main,
And filled the meanest worm that crawls in dust
With spirit, thought, and love; on Man alone,

Queen Mab

Partial in causeless malice, wantonly
Heaped ruin, vice, and slavery; his soul
Blasted with withering curses; placed afar
The meteor-happiness, that shuns his grasp,
But serving on the frightful gulph to glare,
Rent wide beneath his footsteps?

                               Nature ! — no !
Kings, priests, and statesmen, blast the human
    flower
Even in its tender bud; their influence darts
Like subtle poison through the bloodless veins
Of desolate society.   The child,
Ere he can lisp his mother's sacred name,
Swells with the unnatural pride of crime, and
    lifts
His baby-sword even in a hero's mood.
This infant-arm becomes the bloodiest scourge
Of devastated earth; whilst specious names,
Learnt in soft childhood's unsuspecting hour,
Serve as the sophisms with which manhood
    dims
Bright reason's ray, and sanctifies the sword
Upraised to shed a brother's innocent blood.

Queen Mab

Let priest-led slaves cease to proclaim that man
Inherits vice and misery, when force
And falsehood hang even o'er the cradled babe,
Stifling with rudest grasp all natural good.

Ah! to the stranger-soul, when first it peeps
From its new tenement, and looks abroad
For happiness and sympathy, how stern
And desolate a tract is this wide world!
How withered all the buds of natural good!
No shade, no shelter from the sweeping
    storms
Of pitiless power! On its wretched frame,
Poisoned, perchance, by the disease and woe
Heaped on the wretched parent whence it
    sprung
By morals, law, and custom, the pure winds
Of heaven, that renovate the insect tribes,
May breathe not. The untainting light of
    day
May visit not its longings. It is bound
Ere it has life: yea, all the chains are forged
Long ere its being: all liberty and love

Queen Mab

And peace is torn from its defencelessness;
Cursed from its birth, even from its cradle
    doomed
To abjectness and bondage!

Throughout this varied and eternal world
Soul is the only element: the block
That for uncounted ages has remained
The moveless pillar of a mountain's weight
Is active, living spirit.   Every grain
Is sentient both in unity and part,
And the minutest atom comprehends
A world of loves and hatreds; these beget
Evil and good: hence truth and falsehood
    spring;
Hence will and thought and action, all the
    germs
Of pain or pleasure, sympathy or hate,
That variegate the eternal universe.
Soul is not more polluted than the beams
Of heaven's pure orb, ere round their rapid
    lines
The taint of earth-born atmospheres arise.

Queen Mab

Man is of soul and body, formed for deeds
Of high resolve, on fancy's boldest wing
To soar unwearied, fearlessly to turn
The keenest pangs to peacefulness, and taste
The joys which mingled sense and spirit yield.
Or he is formed for abjectness and woe,
To grovel on the dunghill of his fears,
To shrink at every sound, to quench the
    flame
Of natural love in sensualism, to know
That hour as blest when on his worthless
    days
The frozen hand of death shall set its seal,
Yet fear the cure, though hating the disease.
The one is man that shall hereafter be;
The other, man as vice has made him now.

War is the statesman's game, the priest's
    delight,
The lawyer's jest, the hired assassin's trade,
And, to those royal murderers, whose mean
    thrones
Are bought by crimes of treachery and gore,

Queen Mab

The bread they eat, the staff on which they lean.
Guards, garbed in blood-red livery, surround
Their palaces, participate the crimes
That force defends, and from a nation's rage
Secure the crown, which all the curses reach
That famine, frenzy, woe and penury breathe.
These are the hired bravos who defend
The tyrant's throne — the bullies of his fear:
These are the sinks and channels of worst
    vice,
The refuse of society, the dregs
Of all that is most vile: their cold hearts
    blend
Deceit with sternness, ignorance with pride,
All that is mean and villainous with rage
Which hopelessness of good, and self-con-
    tempt,
Alone might kindle; they are decked in
    wealth,
Honour and power, then are sent abroad
To do their work.   The pestilence that stalks
In gloomy triumph through some eastern land
Is less destroying.   They cajole with gold,

Queen Mab

And promises of fame, the thoughtless youth
Already crushed with servitude : he knows
His wretchedness too late, and cherishes
Repentance for his ruin, when his doom
Is sealed in gold and blood!
Those too the tyrant serve, who, skilled to
    snare
The feet of justice in the toils of law,
Stand, ready to oppress the weaker still;
And right or wrong will vindicate for gold,
Sneering at public virtue, which beneath
Their pitiless tread lies torn and trampled,
    where
Honour sits smiling at the sale of truth.

Then grave and hoary-headed hypocrites,
Without a hope, a passion, or a love,
Who, through a life of luxury and lies,
Have crept by flattery to the seats of power,
Support the system whence their honours
    flow. . . .
They have three words : — well tyrants know
    their use,

Queen Mab

Well pay them for the loan, with usury
Torn from a bleeding world!—God, Hell,
    and Heaven.
A vengeful, pitiless, and almighty fiend,
Whose mercy is a nickname for the rage
Of tameless tigers hungering for blood.
Hell, a red gulph of everlasting fire,
Where poisonous and undying worms prolong
Eternal misery to those hapless slaves
Whose life has been a penance for its crimes.
And Heaven, a meed for those who dare belie
Their human nature, quake, believe, and
    cringe
Before the mockeries of earthly power.

These tools the tyrant tempers to his work,
Wields in his wrath, and as he wills destroys,
Omnipotent in wickedness: the while
Youth springs, age moulders, manhood tamely
    does
His bidding, bribed by short-lived joys to
    lend
Force to the weakness of his trembling arm.

Queen Mab

They rise, they fall; one generation comes
Yielding its harvest to destruction's scythe.
It fades, another blossoms: yet behold!
Red glows the tyrant's stamp-mark on its
    bloom,
Withering and cankering deep its passive
    prime.
He has invented lying words and modes,
Empty and vain as his own coreless heart;
Evasive meanings, nothings of much sound,
To lure the heedless victim to the toils
Spread round the valley of its paradise.

Look to thyself, priest, conqueror, or prince!
Whether thy trade is falsehood, and thy lusts
Deep wallow in the earnings of the poor,
With whom thy master was:—or thou de-
    light'st
In numbering o'er the myriads of thy slain,
All misery weighing nothing in the scale
Against thy short-lived fame: or thou dost
    load
With cowardice and crime the groaning land,

A pomp-fed king.   Look to thy wretched
    self!
Aye, art thou not the veriest slave that e'er
Crawled on the loathing earth?   Are not thy
    days
Days of unsatisfying listlessness?
Dost thou not cry, ere night's long rack is
    o'er,
When will the morning come?   Is not thy
    youth
A vain and feverish dream of sensualism?
Thy manhood blighted with unripe disease?
Are not thy views of unregretted death
Drear, comfortless, and horrible?   Thy mind,
Is it not morbid as thy nerveless frame,
Incapable of judgment, hope, or love?
And dost thou wish the errors to survive
That bar thee from all sympathies of good,
After the miserable interest
Thou hold'st in their protraction?   When the
    grave
Has swallowed up thy memory and thyself,
Dost thou desire the bane that poisons earth

Queen Mab

To twine its roots around thy coffined clay,
Spring from thy bones, and blossom on thy
    tomb,
That of its fruit thy babes may eat and die?

V.

HUS do the generations of the
earth
Go to the grave, and issue from
the womb,
Surviving still the imperishable change
That renovates the world; even as the leaves
Which the keen frost-wind of the waning year
Has scattered on the forest soil, and heaped
For many seasons there, though long they
choke,
Loading with loathsome rottenness the land,
All germs of promise, yet when the tall trees
From which they fell, shorn of their lovely
shapes,
Lie level with the earth to moulder there,
They fertilize the land they long deformed,
Till from the breathing lawn a forest springs
Of youth, integrity, and loveliness,

Queen Mab

Like that which gave it life, to spring and die.
Thus suicidal selfishness, that blights
The fairest feelings of the opening heart,
Is destined to decay, whilst from the soil
Shall spring all virtue, all delight, all love,
And judgment cease to wage unnatural war
With passion's unsubduable array.
Twin-sister of religion, selfishness!
Rival in crime and falsehood, aping all
The wanton horrors of her bloody play;
Yet frozen, unimpassioned, spiritless,
Shunning the light, and owning not its name,
Compelled, by its deformity, to screen
With flimsy veil of justice and of right,
Its unattractive lineaments, that scare
All, save the brood of ignorance: at once
The cause and the effect of tyranny;
Unblushing, hardened, sensual, and vile;
Dead to all love but of its abjectness,
With heart impassive by more noble powers
Than unshared pleasure, sordid gain, or fame;
Despising its own miserable being,
Which still it longs, yet fears to disenthrall.

Queen Mab

Hence commerce springs, the venal inter-
   change
Of all that human art or nature yield ;
Which wealth should purchase not, but want
   demand,
And natural kindness hasten to supply
From the full fountain of its boundless love,
For ever stifled, drained, and tainted now.
Commerce ! beneath whose poison-breathing
   shade
No solitary virtue dares to spring,
But poverty and wealth with equal hand
Scatter their withering curses, and unfold
The doors of premature and violent death,
To pining famine and full-fed disease,
To all that shares the lot of human life,
Which poisoned, body and soul, scarce drags
   the chain,
That lengthens as it goes and clanks behind.

Commerce has set the mark of selfishness,
The signet of its all-enslaving power
Upon a shining ore, and called it gold :

Queen Mab

Before whose image bow the vulgar great,
The vainly rich, the miserable proud,
The mob of peasants, nobles, priests, and
    kings,
And with blind feelings reverence the power
That grinds them to the dust of misery.
But in the temple of their hireling hearts
Gold is a living god, and rules in scorn
All earthly things but virtue.

Since tyrants, by the sale of human life,
Heap luxuries to their sensualism, and fame
To their wide-wasting and insatiate pride,
Success has sanctioned to a credulous world
The ruin, the disgrace, the woe of war.
His hosts of blind and unresisting dupes
The despot numbers; from his cabinet
These puppets of his schemes he moves at will,
Even as the slaves by force or famine driven,
Beneath a vulgar master, to perform
A task of cold and brutal drudgery; —
Hardened to hope, insensible to fear,
Scarce living pulleys of a dead machine,

Queen Mab

Mere wheels of work and articles of trade,
That grace the proud and noisy pomp of
    wealth !

The harmony and happiness of man
Yields to the wealth of nations; that which
    lifts
His nature to the heaven of its pride
Is bartered for the poison of his soul ;
The weight that drags to earth his towering
    hopes,
Blighting all prospect but of selfish gain,
Withering all passion but of slavish fear,
Extinguishing all free and generous love
Of enterprise and daring, even the pulse
That fancy kindles in the beating heart
To mingle with sensation, it destroys, —
Leaves nothing but the sordid lust of self,
The grovelling hope of interest and gold,
Unqualified, unmingled, unredeemed
Even by hypocrisy.
            And statesmen boast
Of wealth ! The wordy eloquence, that lives

Queen Mab

After the ruin of their hearts, can gild
The bitter poison of a nation's woe,
Can turn the worship of the servile mob
To their corrupt and glaring idol fame,
From virtue, trampled by its iron tread,
Although its dazzling pedestal be raised
Amid the horrors of a limb-strewn field,
With desolated dwellings smoking round.
The man of ease, who, by his warm fireside,
To deeds of charitable intercourse
And bare fulfilment of the common laws
Of decency and prejudice, confines
The struggling nature of his human heart,
Is duped by their cold sophistry; he sheds
A passing tear perchance upon the wreck
Of earthly peace, when near his dwelling's
    door
The frightful waves are driven, — when his
    son
Is murdered by the tyrant, or religion
Drives his wife raving mad. But the poor
    man,
Whose life is misery, and fear, and care;

Queen Mab

Whom the morn wakens but to fruitless toil;
Who ever hears his famished offspring's
 scream,
Whom their pale mother's uncomplaining
 gaze
For ever meets, and the proud rich man's eye
Flashing command, and the heart-breaking
 scene
Of thousands like himself; — he little heeds
The rhetoric of tyranny; his hate
Is quenchless as his wrongs; he laughs to
 scorn
The vain and bitter mockery of words,
Feeling the horror of the tyrant's deeds,
And unrestrained but by the arm of power,
That knows and dreads his enmity.

The iron rod of penury still compels
Her wretched slave to bow the knee to wealth,
And poison, with unprofitable toil,
A life too void of solace to confirm
The very chains that bind him to his doom.
Nature, impartial in munificence,

Queen Mab

Has gifted man with all-subduing will.
Matter, with all its transitory shapes,
Lies subjected and plastic at his feet,
That, weak from bondage, tremble as they
     tread.
How many a rustic Milton has passed by,
Stifling the speechless longings of his heart,
In unremitting drudgery and care !
How many a vulgar Cato has compelled
His energies, no longer tameless then,
To mould a pin, or fabricate a nail !
How many a Newton, to whose passive ken
Those mighty spheres that gem infinity
Were only specks of tinsel, fixed in heaven
To light the midnights of his native town !

Yet every heart contains perfection's germ : [
The wisest of the sages of the earth,
That ever from the stores of reason drew
Science and truth, and virtue's dreadless tone,
Were but a weak and inexperienced boy,
Proud, sensual, unimpassioned, unimbued
With pure desire and universal love,

Queen Mab

Compared to that high being, of cloudless
 brain,
Untainted passion, elevated will,
Which death (who even would linger long
 in awe
Within his noble presence, and beneath
His changeless eyebeam) might alone subdue.
Him, every slave now dragging through the
 filth
Of some corrupted city his sad life,
Pining with famine, swoln with luxury,
Blunting the keenness of his spiritual sense
With narrow schemings and unworthy cares,
Or madly rushing through all violent crime,
To move the deep stagnation of his soul, —
Might imitate and equal.
                        But mean lust
Has bound its chains so tight around the
 earth,
That all within it but the virtuous man
Is venal : gold or fame will surely reach
The price prefixed by selfishness, to all
But him of resolute and unchanging will;

70

Queen Mab

Whom, nor the plaudits of a servile crowd,
Nor the vile joys of tainting luxury,
Can bribe to yield his elevated soul
To tyranny or falsehood, though they wield
With blood-red hand the sceptre of the world.

All things are sold : the very light of heaven
Is venal ; earth's unsparing gifts of love,
The smallest and most despicable things
That lurk in the abysses of the deep,
All objects of our life, even life itself,
And the poor pittance which the laws allow
Of liberty, the fellowship of man,
Those duties which his heart of human love
Should urge him to perform instinctively,
Are bought and sold as in a public mart
Of undisguising selfishness, that sets
On each its price, the stamp-mark of her reign.
Even love is sold ; the solace of all woe
Is turned to deadliest agony, old age
Shivers in selfish beauty's loathing arms,
And youth's corrupted impulses prepare
A life of horror from the blighting bane

Queen Mab

Of commerce; whilst the pestilence that
    springs
From unenjoying sensualism, has filled
All human life with hydra-headed woes.

Falsehood demands but gold to pay the pangs
Of outraged conscience; for the slavish priest
Sets no great value on his hireling faith:
A little passing pomp, some servile souls,
Whom cowardice itself might safely chain,
Or the spare mite of avarice could bribe
To deck the triumph of their languid zeal,
Can make him minister to tyranny.
More daring crime requires a loftier meed:
Without a shudder, the slave-soldier lends
His arm to murderous deeds, and steels his
    heart,
When the dread eloquence of dying men,
Low mingling on the lonely field of fame,
Assails that nature, whose applause he sells
For the gross blessings of a patriot mob,
For the vile gratitude of heartless kings,
And for a cold world's good word, — viler still!

Queen Mab

There is a nobler glory, which survives
Until our being fades, and, solacing
All human care, accompanies its change;
Deserts not virtue in the dungeon's gloom,
And, in the precincts of the palace, guides
Its footsteps through that labyrinth of crime;
Imbues his lineaments with dauntlessness,
Even when, from power's avenging hand, he
    takes
Its sweetest, last, and noblest title — death;
— The consciousness of good, which neither
    gold,
Nor sordid fame, nor hope of heavenly bliss
Can purchase; but a life of resolute good,
Unalterable will, quenchless desire
Of universal happiness, the heart
That beats with it in unison, the brain,
Whose ever wakeful wisdom toils to change
Reason's rich stores for its eternal weal.

This commerce of sincerest virtue needs
No mediative signs of selfishness,
No jealous intercourse of wretched gain,

Queen Mab

No balancings of prudence, cold and long;
In just and equal measure all is weighed,
One scale contains the sum of human weal,
And one, the good man's heart.

                             How vainly seek
The selfish for that happiness denied
To aught but virtue! Blind and hardened,
    they,
Who hope for peace amid the storms of care,
Who covet power they know not how to use,
And sigh for pleasure they refuse to give, —
Madly they frustrate still their own designs;
And, where they hope that quiet to enjoy
Which virtue pictures, bitterness of soul,
Pining regrets, and vain repentances,
Disease, disgust, and lassitude, pervade
Their valueless and miserable lives.

But hoary-headed selfishness has felt
Its death-blow, and is tottering to the grave:
A brighter morn awaits the human day,
When every transfer of earth's natural gifts
Shall be a commerce of good words and works;

74

Queen Mab

When poverty and wealth, the thirst of fame,
The fear of infamy, disease and woe,
War with its million horrors, and fierce hell
Shall live but in the memory of time,
Who, like a penitent libertine, shall start,
Look back, and shudder at his younger years.

VI.

ALL touch, all eye, all ear,
  The Spirit felt the Fairy's burn-
    ing speech.
  O'er the thin texture of its frame,
The varying periods painted changing glows,
   As on a summer even,
When soul-enfolding music floats around,
  The stainless mirror of the lake
  Reimages the eastern gloom,
Mingling convulsively its purple hues
   With sunset's burnished gold.

   Then thus the Spirit spoke :
It is a wild and miserable world !
   Thorny, and full of care,
Which every fiend can make his prey at will.
  O Fairy ! in the lapse of years,
    Is there no hope in store?

Queen Mab

Will yon vast suns roll on
Interminably, still illuming
The night of so many wretched souls,
     And see no hope for them?
Will not the universal Spirit e'er
Revivify this withered limb of Heaven?

     The Fairy calmly smiled
In comfort, and a kindling gleam of hope
     Suffused the Spirit's lineaments.
Oh! rest thee tranquil; chase those fearful
     doubts,
Which ne'er could rack an everlasting soul,
That sees the chains which bind it to its
     doom.
Yes! crime and misery are in yonder earth,
     Falsehood, mistake, and lust;
     But the eternal world
Contains at once the evil and the cure.
Some eminent in virtue shall start up,
     Even in perversest time:
The truths of their pure lips, that never die,
Shall bind the scorpion falsehood with a wreath

Queen Mab

Of ever-living flame,
Until the monster sting itself to death.

How sweet a scene will earth become !
Of purest spirits a pure dwelling-place,
Symphonious with the planetary spheres;
When man, with changeless nature coalescing,
Will undertake regeneration's work,
When its ungenial poles no longer point
      To the red and baleful sun
      That faintly twinkles there.

      Spirit ! on yonder earth,
. Falsehood now triumphs; deadly power
Has fixed its seal upon the lip of truth !
   Madness and misery are there !
The happiest is most wretched ! Yet confide,
Until pure health-drops, from the cup of joy,
Fall like a dew of balm upon the world.
Now, to the scene I show, in silence turn,
And read the blood-stained charter of all woe,
Which nature soon, with recreating hand,
Will blot in mercy from the book of earth.

Queen Mab

How bold the flight of passion's wandering
    wing,
How swift the step of reason's firmer tread,
How calm and sweet the victories of life,
How terrorless the triumph of the grave!
How powerless were the mightiest monarch's
    arm,
Vain his loud threat, and impotent his frown!
How ludicrous the priest's dogmatic roar!
The weight of his exterminating curse,
How light! and his affected charity,
To suit the pressure of the changing times,
What palpable deceit! — but for thy aid,
Religion! but for thee, prolific fiend,
Who peoplest earth with demons, hell with
    men,
And heaven with slaves!

Thou taintest all thou lookest upon! — the
    stars,
Which on thy cradle beamed so brightly
    sweet,
Were gods to the distempered playfulness

Of thy untutored infancy : the trees,
The grass, the clouds, the mountains, and the
    sea,
All living things that walk, swim, creep, or fly,
Were gods : the sun had homage, and the
    moon
Her worshipper.   Then thou becamest, a boy,
More daring in thy frenzies : every shape,
Monstrous or vast, or beautifully wild,
Which, from sensation's relics, fancy culls ;
The spirits of the air, the shuddering ghost,
The genii of the elements, the powers
That give a shape to nature's varied works,
Had life and place in the corrupt belief
Of thy blind heart : yet still thy youthful
    hands
Were pure of human blood.   Then manhood
    gave
Its strength and ardour to thy frenzied brain ;
Thine eager gaze scanned the stupendous
    scene,
Whose wonders mocked the knowledge of thy
    pride :

Queen Mab

Their everlasting and unchanging laws
Reproached thine ignorance.   Awhile thou
    stood'st
Baffled and gloomy; then thou didst sum up
The elements of all that thou didst know;
The changing seasons, winter's leafless reign,
The budding of the heaven-breathing trees,
The eternal orbs that beautify the night,
The sunrise, and the setting of the moon,
Earthquakes and wars, and poisons and dis-
    ease,
And all their causes, to an abstract point,
Converging, thou didst bend and called it
    God!
The self-sufficing, the omnipotent,
The merciful, and the avenging God!
Who, prototype of human misrule, sits
High in heaven's realm, upon a golden throne,
Even like an earthly king; and whose dread
    work,
Hell, gapes for ever for the unhappy slaves
Of fate, whom he created, in his sport,
To triumph in their torments when they fell!

Queen Mab

Earth heard the name; earth trembled, as the
    smoke
Of his revenge ascended up to heaven,
Blotting the constellations; and the cries
Of millions, butchered in sweet confidence
And unsuspecting peace, even when the bonds
Of safety were confirmed by wordy oaths
Sworn in his dreadful name, rung through the
    land;
Whilst innocent babes writhed on thy stubborn
    spear,
And thou didst laugh to hear the mother's
    shriek
Of maniac gladness, as the sacred steel
Felt cold in her torn entrails!

Religion! thou wert then in manhood's prime:
But age crept on: one God would not suffice
For senile puerility; thou framedst
A tale to suit thy dotage, and to glut
Thy misery-thirsting soul, that the mad fiend
Thy wickedness had pictured might afford
A plea for sating the unnatural thirst

82

Queen Mab

For murder, rapine, violence, and crime,
That still consumed thy being, even when
Thou heard'st the step of fate ; — that flames
    might light
Thy funeral scene, and the shrill horrent shrieks
Of parents dying on the pile that burned
To light their children to thy paths, the roar
Of the encircling flames, the exulting cries
Of thine apostles, loud commingling there,
    Might sate thine hungry ear
    Even on the bed of death !

But now contempt is mocking thy gray hairs ;
Thou art descending to the darksome grave,
Unhonoured and unpitied, but by those
Whose pride is passing by like thine, and sheds,
Like thine, a glare that fades before the sun
Of truth, and shines but in the dreadful night
That long has lowered above the ruined world.

Throughout these infinite orbs of mingling
    light,
Of which yon earth is one, is wide diffused

Queen Mab

A spirit of activity and life,
That knows no term, cessation, or decay;
That fades not when the lamp of earthly life,
Extinguished in the dampness of the grave,
Awhile there slumbers, more than when the
    babe
In the dim newness of its being feels
The impulses of sublunary things,
And all is wonder to unpractised sense:
But, active, steadfast, and eternal, still
Guides the fierce whirlwind, in the tempest
    roars,
Cheers in the day, breathes in the balmy groves,
Strengthens in health, and poisons in disease;
And in the storm of change, that ceaselessly
Rolls round the eternal universe, and shakes
Its undecaying battlement, presides,
Apportioning with irresistible law
The place each spring of its machine shall fill;
So that when waves on waves tumultuous heap
Confusion to the clouds, and fiercely driven
Heaven's lightnings scorch the uprooted ocean-
    fords,

Queen Mab

Whilst, to the eye of shipwrecked mariner,
Lone sitting on the bare and shuddering rock,
All seems unlinked contingency and chance:
No atom of this turbulence fulfils
A vague and unnecessitated task,
Or acts but as it must and ought to act.
Even the minutest molecule of light,
That in an April sunbeam's fleeting glow
Fulfils its destined, though invisible work,
The universal Spirit guides; nor less,
When merciless ambition, or mad zeal,
Has led two hosts of dupes to battle-field,
That, blind, they there may dig each other's
    graves,
And call the sad work glory, does it rule
All passions: not a thought, a will, an act,
No working of the tyrant's moody mind,
Nor one misgiving of the slaves who boast
Their servitude, to hide the shame they feel,
Nor the events enchaining every will,
That from the depths of unrecorded time
Have drawn all-influencing virtue, pass
Unrecognized, or unforeseen by thee,

Queen Mab

Soul of the Universe! eternal spring
Of life and death, of happiness and woe,
Of all that chequers the phantasmal scene
That floats before our eyes in wavering light,
Which gleams but on the darkness of our
      prison,
    Whose chains and massy walls
    We feel, but cannot see.

Spirit of Nature! all-sufficing Power,
Necessity! thou mother of the world!
Unlike the God of human error, thou
Requirest no prayers or praises; the caprice
Of man's weak will belongs no more to thee
Than do the changeful passions of his breast
To thy unvarying harmony: the slave,
Whose horrible lusts spread misery o'er the
      world,
And the good man, who lifts, with virtuous
      pride,
His being, in the sight of happiness,
That springs from his own works; the poison-
      tree,

Queen Mab

Beneath whose shade all life is withered up,
And the fair oak, whose leafy dome affords
A temple where the vows of happy love
Are registered, are equal in thy sight:
No love, no hate thou cherishest; revenge
And favouritism, and worst desire of fame
Thou knowest not: all that the wide world
    contains
Are but thy passive instruments, and thou
Regard'st them all with an impartial eye,
Whose joy or pain thy nature cannot feel,
  Because thou hast not human sense,
  Because thou art not human mind.

Yes! when the sweeping storm of time
Has sung its death-dirge o'er the ruined fanes
And broken altars of the almighty fiend,
Whose name usurps thy honours, and the blood
Through centuries clotted there, has floated
    down
The tainted flood of ages, shalt thou live
Unchangeable! A shrine is raised to thee,
  Which, nor the tempest breath of time,

Queen Mab

Nor the interminable flood,
  Over earth's slight pageant rolling,
    Availeth to destroy, —
The sensitive extension of the world.
  That wondrous and eternal fane,
Where pain and pleasure, good and evil join,
To do the will of strong necessity,
  And life, in multitudinous shapes,
Still pressing forward where no term can be,
  Like hungry and unresting flame
Curls round the eternal columns of its strength.

VII.

 WAS an infant when my mother went
    went
To see an atheist burned.   She
    took me there:
The dark-robed priests were met around the
    pile ;
The multitude was gazing silently ;
And as the culprit passed with dauntless mien,
Tempered disdain in his unaltering eye,
Mixed with a quiet smile, shone calmly forth :
The thirsty fire crept round his manly limbs ;
His resolute eyes were scorched to blindness
    soon ;
His death-pang rent my heart ! the insensate
    mob
Uttered a cry of triumph, and I wept.

Queen Mab

Weep not, child! cried my mother, for that
    man
Has said, There is no God.

FAIRY

                There is no God!
Nature confirms the faith his death-groan
    sealed:
Let heaven and earth, let man's revolving
    race,
His ceaseless generations tell their tale;
Let every part depending on the chain
That links it to the whole, point to the hand
That grasps its term ! let every seed that falls
In silent eloquence unfold its store
Of argument: infinity within,
Infinity without, belie creation;
The exterminable spirit it contains
Is nature's only God; but human pride
Is skilful to invent most serious names
To hide its ignorance.
                The name of God
Has fenced about all crime with holiness,

Queen Mab

Himself the creature of his worshippers,
Whose names and attributes and passions
    change,
Seeva, Buddh, Foh, Jehovah, God, or Lord,
Even with the human dupes who build his
    shrines,
Still serving o'er the war-polluted world
For desolation's watchword; whether hosts
Stain his death-blushing chariot-wheels, as
    on
Triumphantly they roll, whilst Brahmins raise
A sacred hymn to mingle with the groans;
Or countless partners of his power divide
His tyranny to weakness; or the smoke
Of burning towns, the cries of female helpless-
    ness,
Unarmed old age, and youth, and infancy,
Horribly massacred, ascend to heaven
In honour of his name; or, last and worst,
Earth groans beneath religion's iron age,
And priests dare babble of a god of peace,
Even whilst their hands are red with guiltless
    blood,

Queen Mab

Murdering the while, uprooting every germ
Of truth, exterminating, spoiling all,
Making the earth a slaughter-house!

    O Spirit! through the sense
By which thy inner nature was apprised
  Of outward shows, vague dreams have
    rolled,
  And varied reminiscences have waked
    Tablets that never fade;
  All things have been imprinted there,
  The stars, the sea, the earth, the sky,
  Even the unshapeliest lineaments
    Of wild and fleeting visions
      Have left a record there
      To testify of earth.

These are my empire, for to me is given
The wonders of the human world to keep.
And fancy's thin creations to endow
With manner, being, and reality;
Therefore a wondrous phantom, from the
    dreams

Queen Mab

Of human error's dense and purblind faith,
I will evoke, to meet thy questioning.
          Ahasuerus, rise !

          A strange and woe-worn wight
     Arose beside the battlement,
          And stood unmoving there.
His inessential figure cast no shade
     Upon the golden floor ;
His port and mien bore mark of many
     years,
And chronicles of untold ancientness
Were legible within his beamless eye :
     Yet his cheek bore the mark of youth ;
Freshness and vigour knit his manly frame ;
The wisdom of old age was mingled there
     With youth's primeval dauntlessness ;
          And inexpressible woe,
Chastened by fearless resignation, gave
An awful grace to his all-speaking brow.

SPIRIT

Is there a God ?

93

Queen Mab

Is there a God!—aye, an almighty God,
And vengeful as almighty! Once his voice
Was heard on earth: earth shuddered at the
    sound;
The fiery-visaged firmament expressed
Abhorrence, and the grave of nature yawned
To swallow all the dauntless and the good
That dared to hurl defiance at his throne,
Girt as it was with power. None but slaves
Survived,—cold-blooded slaves, who did the
    work
Of tyrannous omnipotence; whose souls
No honest indignation ever urged
To elevated daring, to one deed
Which gross and sensual self did not pollute.
These slaves built temples for the omnipotent
    fiend,
Gorgeous and vast: the costly altars smoked
With human blood, and hideous pæans rung
Through all the long-drawn aisles. A mur-
    derer heard
His voice in Egypt, one whose gifts and arts

94

Queen Mab

Had raised him to his eminence in power,
Accomplice of omnipotence in crime,
And confidant of the all-knowing one.
    These were Jehovah's words.

" From an eternity of idleness
I, God, awoke; in seven days' toil made earth
From nothing; rested, and created man:
I placed him in a paradise, and there
Planted the tree of evil, so that he
Might eat and perish, and my soul procure
Wherewith to sate its malice, and to turn,
Even like a heartless conqueror of the earth,
All misery to my fame.   The race of men
Chosen to my honour, with impunity
May sate the lusts I planted in their heart.
Here I command thee hence to lead them on,
Until, with hardened feet, their conquering
    troops
Wade on the promised soil through woman's
    blood,
And make my name be dreaded through the
    land.

95

Queen Mab

Yet ever-burning flame and ceaseless woe
Shall be the doom of their eternal souls,
With every soul on this ungrateful earth,
Virtuous or vicious, weak or strong, — even all
Shall perish, to fulfil the blind revenge
(Which you, to men, call justice) of their
    God."

       The murderer's brow
Quivered with horror.
             " God omnipotent,
Is there no mercy? must our punishment
Be endless? will long ages roll away,
And see no term?   Oh! wherefore hast thou
    made
In mockery and wrath this evil earth?
Mercy becomes the powerful — be but just:
O God! repent and save."
             " One way remains:
I will beget a son, and he shall bear
The sins of all the world; he shall arise
In an unnoticed corner of the earth,
And there shall die upon a cross, and purge

Queen Mab

The universal crime; so that the few
On whom my grace descends, those who are
     marked
As vessels to the honour of their God,
May credit this strange sacrifice, and save
Their souls alive: millions shall live and die,
Who ne'er shall call upon their Saviour's name,
But, unredeemed, go to the gaping grave.
Thousands shall deem it an old woman's tale,
Such as the nurses frighten babes withal:
These in a gulph of anguish and of flame
Shall curse their reprobation endlessly,
Yet tenfold pangs shall force them to avow,
Even on their beds of torment, where they
     howl,
My honour, and the justice of their doom.
What then avail their virtuous deeds, their
     thoughts
Of purity, with radiant genius bright,
Or lit with human reason's earthly ray?
Many are called, but few will I elect.
Do thou my bidding, Moses!"
                         Even the murderer's cheek

Queen Mab

Was blanched with horror, and his quivering
    lips
Scarce faintly uttered — "O almighty one,
I tremble and obey !"

O Spirit ! centuries have set their seal
On this heart of many wounds, and loaded
    brain,
Since the Incarnate came : humbly he came,
Veiling his horrible Godhead in the shape
Of man, scorned by the world, his name un-
    heard,
Save by the rabble of his native town,
Even as a parish demagogue.   He led
The crowd ; he taught them justice, truth, and
    peace,
In semblance ; but he lit within their souls
The quenchless flames of zeal, and blest the
    sword
He brought on earth to satiate with the blood
Of truth and freedom his malignant soul.
At length his mortal frame was led to death.
I stood beside him : on the torturing cross

Queen Mab

No pain assailed his unterrestrial sense;
And yet he groaned.   Indignantly I summed
The massacres and miseries which his name
Had sanctioned in my country, and I cried,
"Go! go!" in mockery.
A smile of godlike malice reillumined
His fading lineaments. — "I go," he cried,
"But thou shalt wander o'er the unquiet
    earth
Eternally." —— The dampness of the grave
Bathed my imperishable front.   I fell,
And long lay tranced upon the charmèd soil.
When I awoke hell burned within my brain,
Which staggered on its seat; for all around
The mouldering relics of my kindred lay,
Even as the Almighty's ire arrested them,
And in their various attitudes of death
My murdered children's mute and eyeless
    skulls
Glared ghastily upon me.
                                    But my soul,
From sight and sense of the polluting woe
Of tyranny, had long learned to prefer

Queen Mab

Hell's freedom to the servitude of heaven.
Therefore I rose, and dauntlessly began
My lonely and unending pilgrimage,
Resolved to wage unweariable war
With my almighty tyrant, and to hurl
Defiance at his impotence to harm
Beyond the curse I bore.   The very hand
That barred my passage to the peaceful grave
Has crushed the earth to misery, and given
Its empire to the chosen of his slaves.
These have I seen, even from the earliest
    dawn
Of weak, unstable, and precarious power ;
Then preaching peace, as now they practise
    war,
So, when they turned but from the massacre
Of unoffending infidels, to quench
Their thirst for ruin in the very blood
That flowed in their own veins, and pitiless
    zeal
Froze every human feeling, as the wife
Sheathed in her husband's heart the sacred
    steel,

Queen Mab

Even whilst its hopes were dreaming of her
   love;
And friends to friends, brothers to brothers
   stood
Opposed in bloodiest battle-field, and war,
Scarce satiable by fate's last death-draught
   waged,
Drunk from the wine-press of the Almighty's
   wrath;
Whilst the red cross, in mockery of peace,
Pointed to victory!   When the fray was done,
No remnant of the exterminated faith
Survived to tell its ruin, but the flesh,
With putrid smoke poisoning the atmosphere,
That rotted on the half-extinguished pile.

Yes! I have seen God's worshippers unsheathe
The sword of his revenge, when grace de-
   scended,
Confirming all unnatural impulses,
To sanctify their desolating deeds;
And frantic priests waved the ill-omened cross
O'er the unhappy earth; then shone the sun

Queen Mab

On showers of gore from the upflashing steel
Of safe assassination, and all crime
Made stingless by the spirits of the Lord,
And blood-red rainbows canopied the land.

Spirit! no year of my eventful being
Has passed unstained by crime and misery,
Which flows from God's own faith.   I've
    marked his slaves
With tongues whose lies are venomous, be-
    guile
The insensate mob, and, whilst one hand was
    red
With murder, feign to stretch the other out
For brotherhood and peace; and that they
    now
Babble of love and mercy, whilst their deeds
Are marked with all the narrowness and crime
That freedom's young arm dare not yet
    chastise,
Reason may claim our gratitude, who now
Establishing the imperishable throne
Of truth, and stubborn virtue, maketh vain

Queen Mab

The unprevailing malice of my foe,
Whose bootless rage heaps torments for the
    brave,
Adds impotent eternities to pain,
Whilst keenest disappointment racks his breast
To see the smiles of peace around them play,
To frustrate or to sanctify their doom.

Thus have I stood, — through a wild waste of
    years
Struggling with whirlwinds of mad agony,
Yet peaceful, and serene, and self-enshrined,
Mocking my powerless tyrant's horrible curse
With stubborn and unalterable will,
Even as a giant oak, which heaven's fierce
    flame
Had scathèd in the wilderness, to stand
A monument of fadeless ruin there;
Yet peacefully and movelessly it braves
The midnight conflict of the wintry storm,
  As in the sunlight's calm it spreads
  Its worn and withered arms on high
To meet the quiet of a summer's noon.

Queen Mab

The Fairy waved her wand:
Ahasuerus fled
Fast as the shapes of mingled shade and mist,
That lurk in the glens of a twilight grove,
Flee from the morning beam:
The matter of which dreams are made
Not more endowed with actual life
Than this phantasmal portraiture
Of wandering human thought.

VIII.

THE present and the past thou hast
    beheld :
    It was a desolate sight.   Now,
      Spirit, learn
  The secrets of the future. — Time !
Unfold the brooding pinion of thy gloom,
Render thou up thy half-devoured babes,
And from the cradles of eternity,
Where millions lie lulled to their portioned
    sleep
By the deep murmuring stream of passing
    things,
Tear thou that gloomy shroud. — Spirit,
  behold
    Thy glorious destiny !

    Joy to the Spirit came.
Through the wide rent in Time's eternal veil,

Queen Mab

Hope was seen beaming through the mists of
    fear :
        Earth was no longer hell ;
        Love, freedom, health, had given
Their ripeness to the manhood of its prime,
        And all its pulses beat
Symphonious to the planetary spheres :
        Then dulcet music swelled
Concordant with the life-strings of the soul ;
It throbbed in sweet and languid beatings
    there,
Catching new life from transitory death, —
Like the vague sighings of a wind at even,
That wakes the wavelets of the slumbering sea
And dies on the creation of its breath,
And sinks and rises, fails and swells by fits :
        Was the pure stream of feeling
        That sprung from these sweet notes,
And o'er the Spirit's human sympathies
With mild and gentle motion calmly flowed.

    Joy to the Spirit came, —
Such joy as when a lover sees

Queen Mab

The chosen of his soul in happiness,
    And witnesses her peace
Whose woe to him were bitterer than death,
    Sees her unfaded cheek
Glow mantling in first luxury of health,
    Thrills with her lovely eyes,
Which like two stars amid the heaving main
    Sparkle through liquid bliss.

Then in her triumph spoke the Fairy Queen :
I will not call the ghost of ages gone
To unfold the frightful secrets of its lore ;
    The present now is past,
And those events that desolate the earth
Have faded from the memory of Time,
Who dares not give reality to that
Whose being I annul. To me is given
The wonders of the human world to keep,
Space, matter, time, and mind. Futurity
Exposes now its treasure ; let the sight
Renew and strengthen all thy failing hope.
O human Spirit ! spur thee to the goal
Where virtue fixes universal peace,

Queen Mab

And midst the ebb and flow of human things,
Show somewhat stable, somewhat certain still,
A lighthouse o'er the wild of dreary waves.

The habitable earth is full of bliss;
Those wastes of frozen billows that were hurled
By everlasting snow-storms round the poles,
Where matter dared not vegetate or live,
But ceaseless frost round the vast solitude
Bound its broad zone of stillness, are unloosed;
And fragrant zephyrs there from spicy isles
Ruffle the placid ocean-deep, that rolls
Its broad, bright surges to the sloping sand,
Whose roar is wakened into echoings sweet
To murmur through the heaven-breathing
    groves
And melodize with man's blest nature there.

Those deserts of immeasurable sand,
Whose age-collected fervours scarce allowed
A bird to live, a blade of grass to spring,
Where the shrill chirp of the green lizard's
    love

Queen Mab

Broke on the sultry silentness alone,
Now teem with countless rills and shady woods,
Corn-fields and pastures and white cottages;
And where the startled wilderness beheld
A savage conqueror stained in kindred blood,
A tigress sating with the flesh of lambs
The unnatural famine of her toothless cubs,
Whilst shouts and howlings through the desert
    rang,
Sloping and smooth the daisy-spangled lawn,
Offering sweet incense to the sunrise, smiles
To see a babe before his mother's door,
    Sharing his morning's meal
  With the green and golden basilisk
    That comes to lick his feet.

Those trackless deeps, where many a weary
    sail
Has seen above the illimitable plain,
Morning on night, and night on morning rise,
Whilst still no land to greet the wanderer
    spread
Its shadowy mountains on the sun-bright sea,

Queen Mab

Where the loud roarings of the tempest-waves
So long have mingled with the gusty wind
In melancholy loneliness, and swept
The desert of those ocean solitudes,
But vocal to the sea-bird's harrowing shriek,
The bellowing monster, and the rushing storm,
Now to the sweet and many-mingling sounds
Of kindliest human impulses respond.
Those lonely realms bright garden-isles begem,
With lightsome clouds and shining seas be-
      tween,
And fertile valleys, resonant with bliss,
Whilst green woods overcanopy the wave,
Which like a toil-worn labourer leaps to shore,
To meet the kisses of the flowrets there.

All things are recreated, and the flame
Of consentaneous love inspires all life:
The fertile bosom of the earth gives suck
To myriads, who still grow beneath her care,
Rewarding her with their pure perfectness:
The balmy breathings of the wind inhale
Her virtues, and diffuse them all abroad:

Queen Mab

Health floats amid the gentle atmosphere,
Glows in the fruits, and mantles on the stream :
No storms deform the beaming brow of heaven,
Nor scatter in the freshness of its pride
The foliage of the ever-verdant trees ;
But fruits are ever ripe, flowers ever fair,
And autumn proudly bears her matron grace,
Kindling a flush on the fair cheek of spring,
Whose virgin bloom beneath the ruddy fruit
Reflects its tint and blushes into love.

The lion now forgets to thirst for blood :
There might you see him sporting in the sun
Beside the dreadless kid ; his claws are sheathed,
His teeth are harmless, custom's force has
  made
His nature as the nature of a lamb.
Like passion's fruit, the nightshade's tempting
  bane
Poisons no more the pleasure it bestows :
All bitterness is past ; the cup of joy
Unmingled mantles to the goblet's brim,
And courts the thirsty lips it fled before.

But chief, ambiguous man, he that can know
More misery, and dream more joy than all;
Whose keen sensations thrill within his breast
To mingle with a loftier instinct there,
Lending their power to pleasure and to pain,
Yet raising, sharpening, and refining each;
Who stands amid the ever-varying world,
The burthen or the glory of the earth;
He chief perceives the change, his being notes
The gradual renovation, and defines
Each movement of its progress on his mind.

Man, where the gloom of the long polar night
Lowers o'er the snow-clad rocks and frozen
    soil,
Where scarce the hardiest herb that braves the
    frost
Basks in the moonlight's ineffectual glow,
Shrank with the plants, and darkened with the
    night;
His chilled and narrow energies, his heart,
Insensible to courage, truth, or love,
His stunted stature and imbecile frame,

Queen Mab

Marked him for some abortion of the earth,
Fit compeer of the bears that roamed around,
Whose habits and enjoyments were his own:
His life a feverish dream of stagnant woe,
Whose meagre wants, but scantily fulfilled,
Apprised him ever of the joyless length
Which his short being's wretchedness had
    reached;
His death a pang which famine, cold, and toil
Long on the mind, whilst yet the vital spark
Clung to the body stubbornly, had brought:
All was inflicted here that earth's revenge
Could wreak on the infringers of her law;
One curse alone was spared — the name of
    God.

Nor where the tropics bound the realms of
    day
With a broad belt of mingling cloud and flame,
Where blue mists through the unmoving at-
    mosphere
Scattered the seeds of pestilence, and fed
Unnatural vegetation, where the land

Queen Mab

Teemed with all earthquake, tempest, and dis-
    ease,
Was man a nobler being; slavery
Had crushed him to his country's blood-
    stained dust;
Or he was bartered for the fame of power,
Which, all internal impulses destroying,
Makes human will an article of trade;
Or he was changed with Christians for their
    gold,
And dragged to distant isles, where, to the
    sound
Of the flesh-mangling scourge, he does the
    work
Of all-polluting luxury and wealth,
Which doubly visits on the tyrants' heads
The long-protracted fulness of their woe;
Or he was led to legal butchery,
To turn to worms beneath that burning sun,
Where kings first leagued against the rights of
    men,
And priests first traded with the name of
    God.

Queen Mab

Even where the milder zone afforded man
A seeming shelter, yet contagion there,
Blighting his being with unnumbered ills,
Spread like a quenchless fire; nor truth till late
Availed to arrest its progress, or create
That peace which first in bloodless victory
    waved
Her snowy standard o'er this favoured clime:
There man was long the train-bearer of slaves,
The mimic of surrounding misery,
The jackal of ambition's lion-rage,
The bloodhound of religion's hungry zeal.

Here now the human being stands adorning
This loveliest earth with taintless body and
    mind;
Blest from his birth with all bland impulses,
Which gently in his noble bosom wake
All kindly passions and all pure desires.
Him, still from hope to hope the bliss pur-
    suing
Which from the exhaustless lore of human
    weal

Queen Mab

Draws on the virtuous mind, the thoughts that
    rise
In time-destroying infiniteness, gift
With self-enshrined eternity that mocks
The unprevailing hoariness of age,
And man, once fleeting o'er the transient scene
Swift as an unremembered vision, stands
Immortal upon earth : no longer now
He slays the lamb that looks him in the face,
And horribly devours his mangled flesh,
Which, still avenging nature's broken law,
Kindled all putrid humours in his frame,
All evil passions, and all vain belief,
Hatred, despair, and loathing in his mind
The germs of misery, death, disease, and
    crime.
No longer now the wingèd habitants,
That in the woods their sweet lives sing away,
Flee from the form of man ; but gather round,
And prune their sunny feathers on the hands
Which little children stretch in friendly sport
Towards these dreadless partners of their play.
All things are void of terror : man has lost

Queen Mab

His terrible prerogative, and stands
An equal amidst equals : happiness
And science dawn though late upon the earth ;
Peace cheers the mind, health renovates the
    frame ;
Disease and pleasure cease to mingle here,
Reason and passion cease to combat there ;
Whilst each unfettered o'er the earth extend
Their all-subduing energies, and wield
The sceptre of a vast dominion there ;
Whilst every shape and mode of matter lends
Its force to the omnipotence of mind,
Which from its dark mine drags the gem of
    truth
To decorate its paradise of peace.

IX.

HAPPY Earth! reality of
    Heaven!
To which those restless souls
    that ceaselessly
Throng through the human universe, aspire;
Thou consummation of all mortal hope!
Thou glorious prize of blindly-working will!
Whose rays, diffused throughout all space and
    time,
Verge to one point and blend for ever there:
Of purest spirits thou pure dwelling-place!
Where care and sorrow, impotence and crime,
Languor, disease, and ignorance dare not
    come:
O happy Earth, reality of Heaven!

Genius has seen thee in her passionate dreams,
And dim forebodings of thy loveliness,

Queen Mab

Haunting the human heart, have there en-
    twined
Those rooted hopes of some sweet place of
    bliss
Where friends and lovers meet to part no more.
Thou art the end of all desire and will,
The product of all action ; and the souls
That by the paths of an inspiring change
Have reached thy haven of perpetual peace,
There rest from the eternity of toil
That framed the fabric of thy perfectness.

Even Time, the conqueror, fled thee in his
    fear ;
That hoary giant, who, in lonely pride,
So long had ruled the world, that nations fell
Beneath his silent footstep.   Pyramids,
That for millenniums had withstood the tide
Of human things, his storm-breath drove in
    sand
Across that desert where their stones survived
The name of him whose pride had heaped
    them there.

Queen Mab

Yon monarch, in his solitary pomp,
Was but the mushroom of a summer day,
That his light-wingèd footstep pressed to
    dust:
Time was the king of earth: all things gave
    way
Before him, but the fixed and virtuous will,
The sacred sympathies of soul and sense,
That mocked his fury and prepared his fall.

Yet slow and gradual dawned the morn of
    love;
Long lay the clouds of darkness o'er the scene,
Till from its native heaven they rolled away:
First, crime triumphant o'er all hope careered
Unblushing, undisguising, bold and strong;
Whilst falsehood, tricked in virtue's attributes,
Long sanctified all deeds of vice and woe,
Till done by her own venomous sting to
    death,
She left the moral world without a law,
No longer fettering passion's fearless wing,
Nor searing reason with the brand of God.

Queen Mab

Then steadily the happy ferment worked;
Reason was free; and wild though passion
    went
Through tangled glens and wood-embosomed
    meads,
Gathering a garland of the strangest flowers,
Yet like the bee returning to her queen,
She bound the sweetest on her sister's brow,
Who meek and sober kissed the sportive child,
No longer trembling at the broken rod.

Mild was the slow necessity of death:
The tranquil spirit failed beneath its grasp,
Without a groan, almost without a fear,
Calm as a voyager to some distant land,
And full of wonder, full of hope as he.
The deadly germs of languor and disease
Died in the human frame, and purity
Blest with all gifts her earthly worshippers.
How vigorous then the athletic form of age!
How clear its open and unwrinkled brow!
Where neither avarice, cunning, pride, nor
    care,

Queen Mab

Had stamped the seal of gray deformity
On all the mingling lineaments of time.
How lovely the intrepid front of youth!
Which meek-eyed courage decked with fresh-
  est grace;
Courage of soul, that dreaded not a name,
And elevated will, that journeyed on
Through life's phantasmal scene in fearlessness,
With virtue, love, and pleasure, hand in hand.

Then, that sweet bondage which is freedom's
  self,
And rivets with sensation's softest tie
The kindred sympathies of human souls,
Needed no fetters of tyrannic law:
Those delicate and timid impulses
In nature's primal modesty arose,
And with undoubted confidence disclosed
The growing longings of its dawning love,
Unchecked by dull and selfish chastity,
That virtue of the cheaply virtuous,
Who pride themselves in senselessness and
  frost.

Queen Mab

No longer prostitution's venomed bane
Poisoned the springs of happiness and life,
Woman and man, in confidence and love,
Equal and free and pure together trod
The mountain-paths of virtue, which no more
Were stained with blood from many a pil-
　　grim's feet.

Then, where, through distant ages, long in pride
The palace of the monarch-slave had mocked
Famine's faint groan, and penury's silent tear,
A heap of crumbling ruins stood, and threw
Year after year their stones upon the field,
Wakening a lonely echo; and the leaves
Of the old thorn, that on the topmost tower
Usurped the royal ensign's grandeur, shook
In the stern storm that swayed the topmost
　　tower
And whispered strange tales in the whirlwind's
　　ear.

Low through the lone cathedral's roofless aisles
The melancholy winds a death-dirge sung:

Queen Mab

It were a sight of awfulness to see
The works of faith and slavery, so vast,
So sumptuous, yet so perishing withal!
Even as the corpse that rests beneath its wall.
A thousand mourners deck the pomp of death
To-day, the breathing marble glows above
To decorate its memory, and tongues
Are busy of its life : to-morrow, worms
In silence and in darkness seize their prey.

Within the massy prison's mouldering courts,
Fearless and free the ruddy children played,
Weaving gay chaplets for their innocent brows
With the green ivy and the red wallflower,
That mock the dungeon's unavailing gloom ;
The ponderous chains, and gratings of strong
        iron,
There rusted amid heaps of broken stone
That mingled slowly with their native earth :
There the broad beam of day, which feebly
        once
Lighted the cheek of lean captivity
With a pale and sickly glare, then freely shone

Queen Mab

On the pure smiles of infant playfulness :
No more the shuddering voice of hoarse de-
 spair
Pealed through the echoing vaults, but sooth-
 ing notes
Of ivy-fingered winds and gladsome birds
And merriment were resonant around.

These ruins soon left not a wreck behind :
Their elements, wide-scattered o'er the globe,
To happier shapes were moulded, and became
Ministrant to all blissful impulses :
Thus human things were perfected, and earth,
Even as a child beneath its mother's love,
Was strengthened in all excellence, and grew
Fairer and nobler with each passing year.

Now Time his dusky pennons o'er the scene
Closes in steadfast darkness, and the past
Fades from our charmèd sight. My task is
 done :
Thy lore is learned. Earth's wonders are
 thine own,

Queen Mab

With all the fear and all the hope they bring.
My spells are past: the present now recurs.
Ah me! a pathless wilderness remains
Yet unsubdued by man's reclaiming hand.
Yet, human Spirit, bravely hold thy course,
Let virtue teach thee firmly to pursue
The gradual paths of an aspiring change:
For birth and life and death, and that strange
   state
Before the naked soul has found its home,
All tend to perfect happiness, and urge
The restless wheels of being on their way,
Whose flashing spokes, instinct with infinite life,
Bicker and burn to gain their destined goal:
For birth but wakes the spirit to the sense
Of outward shows, whose unexperienced shape
New modes of passion to its frame may lend;
Life is its state of action, and the store
Of all events is aggregated there
That variegate the eternal universe;
Death is a gate of dreariness and gloom,
That leads to azure isles and beaming skies
And happy regions of eternal hope.

Queen Mab

Therefore, O Spirit! fearlessly bear on:
Though storms may break the primrose on its
    stalk,
Though frosts may blight the freshness of its
    bloom,
Yet spring's awakening breath will woo the
    earth,
To feed with kindliest dews its favourite
    flower,
That blooms in mossy banks and darksome
    glens,
Lighting the green wood with its sunny
    smile.

Fear not then, Spirit, death's disrobing hand,
So welcome when the tyrant is awake,
So welcome when the bigot's hell-torch burns;
'Tis but the voyage of a darksome hour,
The transient gulph-dream of a startling sleep.
Death is no foe to virtue: earth has seen
Love's brightest roses on the scaffold bloom,
Mingling with freedom's fadeless laurels there,
And presaging the truth of visioned bliss.

Queen Mab

Are there not hopes within thee, which this
    scene
Of linked and gradual being has confirmed?
Whose stingings bade thy heart look further
    still,
When, to the moonlight walk by Henry led,
Sweetly and sadly thou didst talk of death?
And wilt thou rudely tear them from thy
    breast,
Listening supinely to a bigot's creed,
Or tamely crouching to the tyrant's rod,
Whose iron thongs are red with human gore?
Never: but bravely bearing on, thy will
Is destined an eternal war to wage
With tyranny and falsehood, and uproot
The germs of misery from the human heart.
Thine is the hand whose piety would soothe
The thorny pillow of unhappy crime,
Whose impotence an easy pardon gains,
Watching its wanderings as a friend's disease:
Thine is the brow whose mildness would
    defy
Its fiercest rage, and brave its sternest will,

Queen Mab

When fenced by power and master of the
world.
Thou art sincere and good; of resolute mind,
Free from heart-withering custom's cold con-
trol,
Of passion lofty, pure and unsubdued.
Earth's pride and meanness could not vanquish
thee,
And therefore art thou worthy of the boon
Which thou hast now received: virtue shall
keep
Thy footsteps in the path that thou hast trod,
And many days of beaming hope shall bless
Thy spotless life of sweet and sacred love.
Go, happy one, and give that bosom joy
Whose sleepless spirit waits to catch
Light, life and rapture from thy smile.

The Fairy waves her wand of charm.
Speechless with bliss the spirit mounts the car,
· That rolled beside the battlement,
Bending her beamy eyes in thankfulness.
Again the enchanted steeds were yoked,

Queen Mab

Again the burning wheels inflame
The steep descent of heaven's untrodden way.
    Fast and far the chariot flew:
    The vast and fiery globes that rolled
    Around the Fairy's palace-gate
Lessened by slow degrees and soon appeared
Such tiny twinklers as the planet orbs
That there attendant on the solar power
With borrowed light pursued their narrower
      way.

    Earth floated then below:
    The chariot paused a moment there;
      The Spirit then descended:
The restless coursers pawed the ungenial soil,
Snuffed the gross air, and then, their errand
      done,
Unfurled their pinions to the winds of heaven.

    The Body and the Soul united then,
A gentle start convulsed Ianthe's frame:
Her veiny eyelids quietly unclosed;
Moveless awhile the dark blue orbs remained:

Queen Mab

She looked around in wonder and beheld
Henry, who kneeled in silence by her couch,
Watching her sleep with looks of speechless
love,
And the bright beaming stars
That through the casement shone.

Shelley's Notes

I. — PAGE 17

The sun's unclouded orb
Rolled through the black concave.

BEYOND our atmosphere the sun would appear a rayless orb of fire in the midst of a black concave. The equal diffusion of its light on earth is owing to the refraction of the rays by the atmosphere, and their reflection from other bodies. Light consists either of vibrations propagated through a subtle medium, or of numerous minute particles repelled in all directions from the luminous body. Its velocity greatly exceeds that of any substance with which we are acquainted: observations on the

eclipses of Jupiter's satellites have demonstrated that light takes up no more than 8′ 7″
in passing from the sun to the earth, a distance
of 95,000,000 miles. Some idea may be
gained of the immense distance of the fixed
stars when it is computed that many years
would elapse before light could reach this
earth from the nearest of them; yet in one
year light travels 5,422,400,000,000 miles,
which is a distance 5,707,600 times greater
than that of the sun from the earth.

I. — PAGE 17

Whilst round the chariot's way
Innumerable systems rolled

The plurality of worlds — the indefinite
immensity of the universe — is a most awful
subject of contemplation. He who rightly
feels its mystery and grandeur is in no danger
of seduction from the falsehoods of religious
systems, or of deifying the principle of the
universe. It is impossible to believe that the
Spirit that pervades this infinite machine begat
a son upon the body of a Jewish woman; or

is angered at the consequences of that necessity, which is a synonym of itself. All that miserable tale of the Devil, and Eve, and an Intercessor, with the childish mummeries of the God of the Jews, is irreconcilable with the knowledge of the stars. The works of his fingers have borne witness against him.

The nearest of the fixed stars is inconceivably distant from the earth, and they are probably proportionably distant from each other. By a calculation of the velocity of light, Sirius is supposed to be at least 54,224,-000,000,000 miles from the earth.[1] That which appears only like a thin and silvery cloud streaking the heaven is in effect composed of innumerable clusters of suns, each shining with its own light, and illuminating numbers of planets that revolve around them. Millions and millions of suns are ranged around us, all attended by innumerable worlds, yet calm, regular, and harmonious, all keeping the paths of immutable necessity.

[1] See Nicholson's Encyclopedia, art. Light.

IV. — PAGE 55

These are the hired bravos who defend
The tyrant's throne.

To employ murder as a means of justice is an idea which a man of an enlightened mind will not dwell upon with pleasure. To march forth in rank and file, and all the pomp of streamers and trumpets, for the purpose of shooting at our fellow men as a mark; to inflict upon them all the variety of wound and anguish; to leave them weltering in their blood; to wander over the field of desolation, and count the number of the dying and the dead, — are employments which in thesis we may maintain to be necessary, but which no good man will contemplate with gratulation and delight. A battle we suppose is won : — thus truth is established, thus the cause of justice is confirmed ! It surely requires no common sagacity to discern the connection between this immense heap of calamities and the assertion of truth or the maintenance of justice.

"Kings, and ministers of state, the real

authors of the calamity, sit unmolested in their cabinet, while those against whom the fury of the storm is directed are, for the most part, persons who have been trepanned into the service, or who are dragged unwillingly from their peaceful homes into the field of battle. A soldier is a man whose business it is to kill those who never offended him, and who are the innocent martyrs of other men's iniquities. Whatever may become of the abstract question of the justifiableness of war, it seems impossible that the soldier should not be a depraved and unnatural being.

To these more serious and momentous considerations it may be proper to add a recollection of the ridiculousness of the military character. Its first constituent is obedience: a soldier is, of all descriptions of men, the most completely a machine; yet his profession inevitably teaches him something of dogmatism, swaggering, and self-consequence: he is like the puppet of a showman, who, at the very time he is made to strut and swell and display the most farcical airs, we perfectly know cannot assume the most insignificant gesture, advance either to the right or the left, but as he is moved by his exhibitor." — *Godwin's Enquirer, Essay v.*

I will here subjoin a little poem, so strongly expressive of my abhorrence of despotism and falsehood, that I fear lest it never again may be depictured so vividly. This opportunity is perhaps the only one that ever will occur of rescuing it from oblivion.

FALSEHOOD AND VICE

A DIALOGUE

Whilst monarchs laughed upon their thrones
To hear a famished nation's groans,
And hugged the wealth wrung from the woe
That makes its eyes and veins o'erflow, —
Those thrones, high built upon the heaps
Of bones where frenzied famine sleeps,
Where slavery wields her scourge of iron,
Red with mankind's unheeded gore,
And war's mad fiends the scene environ,
Mingling with shrieks a drunken roar,
There Vice and Falsehood took their stand,
High raised above the unhappy land.

FALSEHOOD

Brother ! arise from the dainty fare,
Which thousands have toiled and bled to bestow ;

Notes to Queen Mab

A finer feast for thy hungry ear
Is the news that I bring of human woe

VICE

And, secret one, what hast thou done,
To compare, in thy tumid pride, with me ?
I, whose career, through the blasted year,
Has been tracked by despair and agony.

FALSEHOOD

What have I done ! — I have torn the robe
From baby truth's unsheltered form,
And round the desolated globe
Borne safely the bewildering charm :
My tyrant-slaves to a dungeon-floor
Have bound the fearless innocent,
And streams of fertilizing gore
Flow from her bosom's hideous rent,
Which this unfailing dagger gave. . . .
I dread that blood ! — no more — this day
Is ours, though her eternal ray
    Must shine upon our grave.
Yet know, proud Vice, had I not given
To thee the robe I stole from heaven,
Thy shape of ugliness and fear
Had never gained admission here

VICE

And know, that had I disdained to toil,
But sate in my loathsome cave the while,

138

Notes to Queen Mab

And ne'er to these hateful sons of heaven,
GOLD, MONARCHY, and MURDER, given;
Hadst thou with all thine art essayed
One of thy games then to have played,
With all thine overweening boast,
Falsehood! I tell thee thou hadst lost! —
Yet wherefore this dispute? — we tend,
Fraternal, to one common end;
In this cold grave beneath my feet,
Will our hopes, our fears, and our labours, meet.

FALSEHOOD

I brought my daughter, RELIGION, on earth:
She smothered Reason's babes in their birth;
But dreaded their mother's eye severe, —
So the crocodile slunk off slily in fear,
And loosed her bloodhounds from the den. . . .
They started from dreams of slaughtered men,
And, by the light of her poison eye,
Did her work o'er the wide earth frightfully:
The dreadful stench of her torches' flare,
Fed with human fat, polluted the air.
The curses, the shrieks, the ceaseless cries
Of the many-mingling miseries,
As on she trod, ascended high
And trumpeted my victory! —
Brother, tell what thou hast done.

VICE

I have extinguished the noonday sun,
In the carnage-smoke of battles won:

Notes to Queen Mab

Famine, murder, hell and power
Were glutted in that glorious hour
Which searchless fate had stamped for me
With the seal of her security. . . .
For the bloated wretch on yonder throne
Commanded the bloody fray to rise.
Like me he joyed at the stifled moan
Wrung from a nation's miseries ;
While the snakes, whose slime even him *defiled*,
In ecstasies of malice smiled :
They thought 'twas theirs, — but mine the deed !
Theirs is the toil, but mine the meed —
Ten thousand victims madly bleed.
They dream that tyrants goad them there
With poisonous war to taint the air :
These tyrants, on their beds of thorn,
Swell with the thoughts of murderous fame,
And with their gains to lift my name
Restless they plan from night to morn :
I — I do all ; without my aid
Thy daughter, that relentless maid,
Could never o'er a death-bed urge
The fury of her venomed scourge.

FALSEHOOD

Brother, well : the world is ours ;
And whether thou or I have won,
The pestilence expectant lours
On all beneath yon blasted sun.
Our joys, our toils, our honours meet
In the milk-white and wormy winding-sheet :

Notes to Queen Mab

A short-lived hope, unceasing care,
Some heartless scraps of godly prayer,
A moody curse, and a frenzied sleep
Ere gapes the grave's unclosing deep,
A tyrant's dream, a coward's start,
The ice that clings to a priestly heart,
A judge's frown, a courtier's smile,
Make the great whole for which we toil ;
And, brother, whether thou or I
Have done the work of misery,
It little boots . thy toil and pain,
Without my aid, were more than vain ;
And but for thee I ne'er had sate
The guardian of heaven's palace gate.

V. — PAGE 62

Thus do the generations of the earth
Go to the grave, and issue from the womb.

One generation passeth away and another
generation cometh, but the earth abideth for
ever.   The sun also ariseth and the sun goeth
down, and hasteth to his place where he arose.
The wind goeth toward the south and turn-
eth about unto the north, it whirleth about
continually, and the wind returneth again according to his circuits.   All the rivers run into

the sea, yet the sea is not full ; unto the place whence the rivers come, thither shall they return again. — *Ecclesiastes*, Chap. i.

V. — PAGE 66

And statesmen boast
Of wealth !

There is no real wealth but the labour of man. Were the mountains of gold and the valleys of silver, the world would not be one grain of corn the richer; no one comfort would be added to the human race. In consequence of our consideration for the precious metals, one man is enabled to heap to himself luxuries at the expense of the necessaries of his neighbour; a system admirably fitted to produce all the varieties of disease and crime, which never fail to characterize the two extremes of opulence and penury. A speculator takes pride to himself as the promoter of his country's prosperity, who employs a number of hands in the manufacture of articles avowedly destitute of use, or subservient only to the unhallowed cravings of luxury and ostentation.

Notes to Queen Mab

The nobleman, who employs the peasants of his neighbourhood in building his palaces, until "*jam pauca aratro jugera regiæ moles relinquunt,*" flatters himself that he has gained the title of a patriot by yielding to the impulses of vanity. The show and pomp of courts adduce the same apology for its continuance; and many a fête has been given, many a woman has eclipsed her beauty by her dress, to benefit the labouring poor and to encourage trade. Who does not see that this is a remedy which aggravates whilst it palliates the countless diseases of society? The poor are set to labour, — for what? Not the food for which they famish: not the blankets for want of which their babes are frozen by the cold of their miserable hovels: not those comforts of civilization without which civilized man is far more miserable than the meanest savage; oppressed as he is by all its insidious evils, within the daily and taunting prospect of its innumerable benefits assiduously exhibited before him: — no; for the pride of power, for the miserable isolation of pride, for the false pleasures of the hundredth part of society. No greater evidence is afforded of the wide extended and radical mistakes of civilized man than this fact: those arts which are essential to his very being are held in the greatest contempt; employments are lucrative in an inverse ratio to their usefulness:[1] the jeweller, the toyman, the actor, gains fame and wealth by the exercise of his useless and ridiculous art; whilst the cultivator of the earth, he without whom society must cease to subsist, struggles through contempt and penury, and perishes by that famine which but for his unceasing exertions would annihilate the rest of mankind.

I will not insult common sense by insisting on the doctrine of the natural equality of man. The question is not concerning its desirableness, but its practicability: so far as it is practicable, it is desirable. That state of human society which approaches nearer to an equal partition of its benefits and evils should, *cæteris paribus*, be preferred: but so long as we conceive that a wanton expenditure of human labour, not for the necessities, not even for the luxuries of the mass of society, but for the egotism and ostentation of a few of its members, is defensible on the ground of public

[1] See Rousseau, *De l'Inégalité parmi les Hommes*, note 7.

justice, so long we neglect to approximate to the redemption of the human race.

Labour is required for physical, and leisure for moral, improvement: from the former of these advantages the rich, and from the latter the poor, by the inevitable conditions of their respective situations, are precluded. A state which should combine the advantages of both would be subjected to the evils of neither. He that is deficient in firm health, or vigorous intellect, is but half a man: hence it follows that to subject the labouring classes to unnecessary labour is wantonly depriving them of any opportunities of intellectual improvement; and that the rich are heaping up for their own mischief the disease, lassitude, and ennui by which their existence is rendered an intolerable burthen.

English reformers exclaim against sinecures, —but the true pension list is the rent-roll of the landed proprietors: wealth is a power usurped by the few, to compel the many to labour for their benefit. The laws which support this system derive their force from the ignorance and credulity of its victims: they are the result of a conspiracy of the few against the many, who are themselves obliged to purchase this preëminence by the loss of all real comfort.

" The commodities that substantially contribute to the subsistence of the human species form a very short catalogue: they demand from us but a slender portion of industry. If these only were produced, and sufficiently produced, the species of man would be continued. If the labour necessarily required to produce them were equitably divided among the poor, and, still more, if it were equitably divided among all, each man's share of labour would be light, and his portion of leisure would be ample. There was a time when this leisure would have been of small comparative value: it is to be hoped that the time will come when it will be applied to the most important purposes. Those hours which are not required for the production of the necessaries of life may be devoted to the cultivation of the understanding, the enlarging our stock of knowledge, the refining our taste, and thus opening to us new and more exquisite sources of enjoyment.

. . . .

146

Notes to Queen Mab

" It was perhaps necessary that a period of monopoly and oppression should subsist, before a period of cultivated equality could subsist. Savages perhaps would never have been excited to the discovery of truth and the invention of art but by the narrow motives which such a period affords. But surely, after the savage state has ceased, and men have set out in the glorious career of discovery and invention, monopoly and oppression cannot be necessary to prevent them from returning to a state of barbarism." — *Godwin's Enquirer, Essay ii.* See also " Pol. Jus ," Book VIII., Chap. ii.

It is a calculation of this admirable author, that all the conveniences of civilized life might be produced, if society would divide the labour equally among its members, by each individual being employed in labour two hours during the day.

V. — PAGE. 67

or religion
Drives his wife raving mad.

I am acquainted with a lady of considerable accomplishments, and the mother of a numerous family, whom the Christian religion has goaded to incurable insanity. A parallel case is, I believe, within the experience of every physician.

" Nam jam sæpe homines patriam, carosque parentes
Prodiderunt, vitare Acherusia templa petentes.''
—*Lucretius.*

V. — PAGE 71

Even love is sold.

Not even the intercourse of the sexes is exempt from the despotism of positive institution. Law pretends even to govern the indisciplinable wanderings of passion, to put fetters on the clearest deductions of reason, and, by appeals to the will, to subdue the involuntary affections of our nature. Love is inevitably consequent upon the perception of loveliness. Love withers under constraint: its very essence is liberty: it is compatible neither with obedience, jealousy, nor fear: it is there most pure, perfect, and unlimited, where its votaries live in confidence, equality, and unreserve.

How long, then, ought the sexual connection to last? what law ought to specify the extent of the grievances which should limit its duration? A husband and wife ought to continue so long united as they love each other: any law which should bind them to cohabitation for one moment after the decay of their affection would be a most intolerable tyranny, and the most unworthy of toleration. How odious an usurpation of the right of private judgment should that law be considered which should make the ties of friendship indissoluble, in spite of the caprices, the inconstancy, the fallibility, and capacity for improvement of the human mind. And by so much would the fetters of love be heavier and more unendurable than those of friendship, as love is more vehement and capricious, more dependent on those delicate peculiarities of imagination, and less capable of reduction to the ostensible merits of the object.

The state of society in which we exist is a mixture of feudal savageness and imperfect civilization. The narrow and unenlightened morality of the Christian religion is an aggravation of these evils. It is not even until lately that mankind have admitted that happi-

ness is the sole end of the science of ethics, as
of all other sciences ; and that the fanatical idea
of mortifying the flesh for the love of God has
been discarded. I have heard, indeed, an
ignorant collegian adduce, in favour of Christianity, its hostility to every worldly feeling ! [1]

But if happiness be the object of morality,
of all human unions and disunions; if the
worthiness of every action is to be estimated
by the quantity of pleasurable sensation it is
calculated to produce, then the connection of
the sexes is so long sacred as it contributes to
the comfort of the parties, and is naturally
dissolved when its evils are greater than its
benefits. There is nothing immoral in this
separation. Constancy has nothing virtuous
in itself, independently of the pleasure it con-
fers, and partakes of the temporizing spirit of

---

[1] The first Christian emperor made a law by which seduction
was punished with death; if the female pleaded her own consent, she also was punished with death, if the parents endeavoured to screen the criminals, they were banished and their
estates were confiscated, the slaves who might be accessory were
burned alive, or forced to swallow melted lead The very offspring of an illegal love were involved in the consequences of
the sentence — *Gibbon's Decline and Fall, etc, Vol 11 , page 210*
See also, for the hatred of the primitive Christians to love and
even marriage, p 269

vice in proportion as it endures tamely moral defects of magnitude in the object of its indiscreet choice. Love is free: to promise for ever to love the same woman is not less absurd than to promise to believe the same creed: such a vow, in both cases, excludes us from all inquiry. The language of the votarist is this: The woman I now love may be infinitely inferior to many others; the creed I now profess may be a mass of errors and absurdities; but I exclude myself from all future information as to the amiability of the one and the truth of the other, resolving blindly, and in spite of conviction, to adhere to them. Is this the language of delicacy and reason? Is the love of such a frigid heart of more worth than its belief?

The present system of constraint does no more, in the majority of instances, than make hypocrites or open enemies. Persons of delicacy and virtue, unhappily united to one whom they find it impossible to love, spend the loveliest season of their life in unproductive efforts to appear otherwise than they are, for the sake of the feelings of their partner or the welfare of their mutual offspring: those of less generosity

and refinement openly avow their disappointment, and linger out the remnant of that union,
which only death can dissolve, in a state of
incurable bickering and hostility. The early
education of their children takes its colour from
the squabbles of the parents; they are nursed
in a systematic school of ill-humour, violence,
and falsehood. Had they been suffered to
part at the moment when indifference rendered
their union irksome, they would have been
spared many years of misery: they would
have connected themselves more suitably, and
would have found that happiness in the society
of more congenial partners which is for ever
denied them by the despotism of marriage.
They would have been separately useful and
happy members of society, who, whilst united,
were miserable and rendered misanthropical by
misery. The conviction that wedlock is indissoluble holds out the strongest of all tempta-
tions to the perverse: they indulge without
restraint in acrimony, and all the little tyran-
nies of domestic life, when they know that
their victim is without appeal. If this connection were put on a rational basis, each would
be assured that habitual ill-temper would ter-

minate in separation, and would check this vicious and dangerous propensity.

Prostitution is the legitimate offspring of marriage and its accompanying errors. Women, for no other crime than having followed the dictates of a natural appetite, are driven with fury from the comforts and sympathies of society. It is less venial than murder; and the punishment which is inflicted on her who destroys her child to escape reproach is lighter than the life of agony and disease to which the prostitute is irrecoverably doomed. Has a woman obeyed the impulse of unerring nature;—society declares war against her, pitiless and eternal war: she must be the tame slave, she must make no reprisals; theirs is the right of persecution, hers the duty of endurance. She lives a life of infamy: the loud and bitter laugh of scorn scares her from all return. She dies of long and lingering disease; yet *she* is in fault, *she* is the criminal, *she* the froward and untamable child,—and society, forsooth, the pure and virtuous matron, who casts her as an abortion from her undefiled bosom! Society avenges herself on the criminals of her own creation; she is employed in anathematizing the vice to-day, which yesterday she was the most zealous to teach. Thus is formed one-tenth of the population of London; meanwhile the evil is twofold. Young men, excluded by the fanatical idea of chastity from the society of modest and accomplished women, associate with these vicious and miserable beings, destroying thereby all those exquisite and delicate sensibilities whose existence cold-hearted worldlings have denied; annihilating all genuine passion, and debasing that to a selfish feeling which is the excess of generosity and devotedness. Their body and mind alike crumble into a hideous wreck of humanity; idiotcy and disease become perpetuated in their miserable offspring, and distant generations suffer for the bigoted morality of their forefathers. Chastity is a monkish and evangelical superstition, a greater foe to natural temperance even than unintellectual sensuality; it strikes at the root of all domestic happiness, and consigns more than half of the human race to misery, that some few may monopolize according to law. A system could not well have been devised more studiously hostile to human happiness than marriage.

Notes to Queen Mab

I conceive that from the abolition of marriage, the fit and natural arrangement of sexual connection would result. I by no means assert that the intercourse would be promiscuous: on the contrary, it appears, from the relation of parent to child, that this union is generally of long duration, and marked above all others with generosity and self-devotion. But this is a subject which it is perhaps premature to discuss. That which will result from the abolition of marriage will be natural and right; because choice and change will be exempted from restraint.

In fact, religion and morality, as they now stand, compose a practical code of misery and servitude: the genius of human happiness must tear every leaf from the accursed book of God ere man can read the inscription on his heart. How would morality, dressed up in stiff stays and finery, start from her own disgusting image should she look in the mirror of nature!

VI. — PAGE 78

To the red and baleful sun
That faintly twinkles there.

The north polar star, to which the axis of the earth, in its present state of obliquity, points. It is exceedingly probable, from many considerations, that this obliquity will gradually diminish, until the equator coincides with the ecliptic: the nights and days will then become equal on the earth throughout the year, and probably the seasons also. There is no great extravagance in presuming that the progress of the perpendicularity of the poles may be as rapid as the progress of intellect; or that there should be a perfect identity between the moral and physical improvement of the human species. It is certain that wisdom is not compatible with disease, and that, in the present state of the climates of the earth, health, in the true and comprehensive sense of the word, is out of the reach of civilized man. Astronomy teaches us that the earth is now in its progress, and that the poles are every year becoming more and more perpendicular to the ecliptic. The strong evidence afforded by the history of mythology, and geological researches, that some event of this nature has taken place already, affords a strong presumption that this progress is not merely an oscillation, as has been surmised by some late astronomers. Bones of animals peculiar to the torrid zone have been found in the north of Siberia, and on the banks of the river Ohio. Plants have been found in the fossil state in the interior of Germany, which demand the present climate of Hindostan for their production. The researches of M. Bailly establish the existence of a people who inhabited a tract in Tartary 49° north latitude, of greater antiquity than either the Indians, the Chinese, or the Chaldeans, from whom these nations derived their sciences and theology. We find, from the testimony of ancient writers, that Britain, Germany, and France were much colder than at present, and that their great rivers were annually frozen over. Astronomy teaches us also that since this period the obliquity of the earth's position has been considerably diminished.

VI. — PAGE 86

Necessity! thou mother of the world!

He who asserts the doctrine of Necessity means that, contemplating the events which compose the moral and material universe, he beholds only an immense and uninterrupted chain of causes and effects, no one of which could occupy any other place than it does occupy, or act in any other place than it does act. The idea of necessity is obtained by our experience of the connection between objects, the uniformity of the operations of nature, the constant conjunction of similar events, and the consequent inference of one from the other. Mankind are therefore agreed in the admission of necessity, if they admit that these two circumstances take place in voluntary action. Motive is to voluntary action in the human mind what cause is to effect in the material universe. The word liberty, as applied to mind, is analogous to the word chance as applied to matter: they spring from an ignorance of the certainty of the conjunction of antecedents and consequents.

Every human being is irresistibly impelled to act precisely as he does act: in the eternity which preceded his birth a chain of causes was generated, which, operating under the name of motives, make it impossible that any thought of his mind, or any action of his life, should be otherwise than it is. Were the doctrine of Necessity false, the human mind would no longer be a legitimate object of science; from like causes it would be in vain that we should expect like effects; the strongest motive would no longer be paramount over the conduct; all knowledge would be vague and undeterminate; we could not predict with any certainty that we might not meet as an enemy to-morrow him with whom we have parted in friendship to-night; the most probable inducements and the clearest reasonings would lose the invariable influence they possess. The contrary of this is demonstrably the fact. Similar circumstances produce the same unvariable effects. The precise character and motives of any man on any occasion being given, the moral philosopher could predict his actions with as much certainty as the natural philosopher could predict the effects of the mixture of any particular chemical substances. Why is the aged husbandman more experienced than the young beginner? Because there is a uniform, undeniable necessity in the operations of the material universe. Why is the old statesman more skilful than the raw politician? Because, relying on the necessary conjunction of motive and action, he proceeds to produce moral effects, by the application of those moral causes which experience has shown to be effectual. Some actions may be found to which we can attach no motives, but these are the effects of causes with which we are unacquainted. Hence the relation which motive bears to voluntary action is that of cause to effect; nor, placed in this point of view, is it, or ever has it been, the subject of popular or philosophical dispute. None but the few fanatics who are engaged in the herculean task of reconciling the justice of their God with the misery of man, will longer outrage common sense by the supposition of an event without a cause, a voluntary action without a motive. History, politics, morals, criticism, all grounds of reasonings, all principles of science, alike assume the truth of the doctrine of Necessity. No farmer carrying his corn to market doubts the sale of it at the market price. The master of a manufactory no more doubts that he can purchase the human labour necessary for his purposes than that his machinery will act as they have been accustomed to act.

But, whilst none have scrupled to admit necessity as influencing matter, many have disputed its dominion over mind. Independently of its militating with the received ideas of the justice of God, it is by no means obvious to a superficial inquiry. When the mind observes its own operations, it feels no connection of motive and action: but as we know "nothing more of causation than the constant conjunction of objects and the consequent inference of one from the other, as we find that these two circumstances are universally allowed to have place in voluntary action, we may be easily led to own that they are subjected to the necessity common to all causes." The actions of the will have a regular conjunction with circumstances and characters; motive is to voluntary action what cause is to effect. But the only idea we can form of causation is a constant conjunction of similar objects, and the consequent inference of one from the other: wherever this is the case necessity is clearly established.

The idea of liberty, applied metaphorically to the will, has sprung from a misconception of the meaning of the word power. What is power? — *id quod potest*, that which can produce any given effect. To deny power is to say that nothing can or has the power to be or act. In the only true sense of the word power, it applies with equal force to the loadstone as to the human will. Do you think these motives, which I shall present, are powerful enough to rouse him? is a question just as common as, Do you think this lever has the power of raising this weight? The advocates of free-will assert that the will has the power of refusing to be determined by the strongest motive: but the strongest motive is that which, overcoming all others, ultimately prevails; this assertion therefore amounts to a denial of the will being ultimately determined by that motive which does determine it, which is absurd. But it is equally certain that a man cannot resist the strongest motive as that he cannot overcome a physical impossibility.

The doctrine of Necessity tends to introduce a great change into the established notions of morality, and utterly to destroy religion. Reward and punishment must be considered, by the Necessarian, merely as motives which he would employ in order to procure the adoption or abandonment of any given line of conduct. Desert, in the present sense of the word, would no longer have any meaning; and he who should inflict pain upon another for no better reason than that he deserved it, would only gratify his revenge under pretence of satisfying justice. It is not enough, says the advocate of free-will, that a criminal should be prevented from a repetition of his crime: he should feel pain, and his torments, when justly inflicted, ought precisely to be proportioned to his fault. But utility is morality; that which is incapable of producing happiness is useless; and though the crime of Damiens must be condemned, yet the frightful torments which revenge, under the name of justice, inflicted on this unhappy man cannot be supposed to have augmented, even at the long run, the stock of pleasurable sensation in the world. At the same time, the doctrine of Necessity does not in the least diminish our disapprobation of vice. The conviction which all feel that a viper is a poisonous animal, and that a tiger is constrained, by the inevitable condition of his existence, to devour men, does not induce us to avoid them less sedulously, or, even more, to hesitate in destroying them : but he would surely be of a hard heart who, meeting with a serpent on a desert island, or in a situation where it was incapable of injury, should wantonly deprive it of existence. A Necessarian is inconsequent to his own principles if he indulges in hatred or contempt; the compassion which he feels for the criminal is unmixed with a desire of injuring him : he looks with an elevated and dreadless composure upon the links of the universal chain as they pass before his eyes; whilst cowardice, curiosity, and inconsistency only assail him in proportion to the feebleness and indistinctness with which he has perceived and rejected the delusions of free-will.

Religion is the perception of the relation in which we stand to the principle of the universe.

But if the principle of the universe be not an organic being, the model and prototype of man, the relation between it and human beings is absolutely none. Without some insight into its will respecting our actions religion is nugatory and vain. But will is only a mode of animal mind; moral qualities also are such as only a human being can possess; to attribute them to the principle of the universe is to annex to it properties incompatible with any possible definition of its nature. It is probable that the word God was originally only an expression denoting the unknown cause of the known events which men perceived in the universe. By the vulgar mistake of a metaphor for a real being, of a word for a thing, it became a man, endowed with human qualities and governing the universe as an earthly monarch governs his kingdom. Their addresses to this imaginary being, indeed, are much in the same style as those of subjects to a king. They acknowledge his benevolence, deprecate his anger, and supplicate his favour.

But the doctrine of Necessity teaches us that in no case could any event have happened otherwise than it did happen, and that, if God

is the author of good, he is also the author of
evil; that, if he is entitled to our gratitude for
the one, he is entitled to our hatred for the
other; that, admitting the existence of this
hypothetic being, he is also subjected to the
dominion of an immutable necessity. It is
plain that the same arguments which prove that
God is the author of food, light, and life, prove
him also to be the author of poison, darkness,
and death. The wide-wasting earthquake, the
storm, the battle, and the tyranny, are attributable to this hypothetic being in the same
degree as the fairest forms of nature, sunshine,
liberty, and peace.

But we are taught, by the doctrine of Necessity, that there is neither good nor evil in the
universe, otherwise than as the events to which
we apply these epithets have relation to our
own peculiar mode of being. Still less than
with the hypothesis of a God will the doctrine
of Necessity accord with the belief of a future
state of punishment. God made man such as
he is, and then damned him for being so: for
to say that God was the author of all good,
and man the author of all evil, is to say
that one man made a straight line and a

crooked one, and another man made the incongruity.

A Mahometan story, much to the present purpose, is recorded, wherein Adam and Moses are introduced disputing before God in the following manner. Thou, says Moses, art Adam, whom God created, and animated with the breath of life, and caused to be worshipped by the angels, and placed in Paradise, from whence mankind have been expelled for thy fault. Whereto Adam answered, Thou art Moses, whom God chose for his apostle, and entrusted with his word, by giving thee the tables of the law, and whom he vouchsafed to admit to discourse with himself. How many years dost thou find the law was written before I was created? Says Moses, Forty. And dost thou not find, replied Adam, these words therein, And Adam rebelled against his Lord and transgressed? Which Moses confessing, Dost thou therefore blame me, continued he, for doing that which God wrote of me that I should do, forty years before I was created, nay, for what was decreed concerning me fifty thousand years before the creation of heaven and earth? —*Sale's Prelim. Disc. to the Koran, p. 164.*

VII. — PAGE 90

There is no God!

This negation must be understood solely to affect a creative Deity. The hypothesis of a pervading Spirit coeternal with the universe remains unshaken.

A close examination of the validity of the proofs adduced to support any proposition is the only secure way of attaining truth, on the advantages of which it is unnecessary to descant: our knowledge of the existence of a Deity is a subject of such importance that it cannot be too minutely investigated; in consequence of this conviction we proceed briefly and impartially to examine the proofs which have been adduced. It is necessary first to consider the nature of belief.

When a proposition is offered to the mind, it perceives the agreement or disagreement of the ideas of which it is composed. A perception of their agreement is termed *belief*. Many obstacles frequently prevent this perception from being immediate; these the mind attempts to remove in order that the perception may be distinct. The mind is active in the investigation in order to perfect the state of perception of the relation which the component ideas of the proposition bear to each, which is passive : the investigation being confused with the perception has induced many falsely to imagine that the mind is active in belief, — that belief is an act of volition, — in consequence of which it may be regulated by the mind. Pursuing, continuing this mistake, they have attached a degree of criminality to disbelief; of which, in its nature, it is incapable : it is equally incapable of merit.

Belief, then, is a passion, the strength of which, like every other passion, is in precise proportion to the degrees of excitement.

The degrees of excitement are three.

The senses are the sources of all knowledge to the mind ; consequently their evidence claims the strongest assent.

The decision of the mind, founded upon our own experience, derived from these sources, claims the next degree.

The experience of others, which addresses itself to the former one, occupies the lowest degree.

(A graduated scale, on which should be marked the capabilities of propositions to approach to the test of the senses, would be a just barometer of the belief which ought to be attached to them.) •

Consequently no testimony can be admitted which is contrary to reason; reason is founded on the evidence of our senses.

Every proof may be referred to one of these three divisions: it is to be considered what arguments we receive from each of them, which should convince us of the existence of a Deity.

1st, The evidence of the senses. If the Deity should appear to us, if he should convince our senses of his existence, this revelation would necessarily command belief. Those to whom the Deity has thus appeared have the strongest possible conviction of his existence. But the God of Theologians is incapable of local visibility.

2d, Reason. It is urged that man knows that whatever is must either have had a beginning, or have existed from all eternity: he also knows that whatever is not eternal must have had a cause. When this reasoning is applied to the universe, it is necessary to prove that it

was created : until that is clearly demonstrated
we may reasonably suppose that it has endured
from all eternity. We must prove design before we can infer a designer. The only idea
which we can form of causation is derivable
from the constant conjunction of objects, and
the consequent inference of one from the other.
In a case where two propositions are diamet-
rically opposite, the mind believes that which
is least incomprehensible ; — it is easier to suppose that the universe has existed from all
eternity than to conceive a being beyond its
limits capable of creating it : if the mind sinks
beneath the weight of one, is it an alleviation
to increase the intolerability of the burthen ?

The other argument, which is founded
on a man's knowledge of his own existence,
stands thus. A man knows not only that he
now is, but that once he was not ; consequently
there must have been a cause. But our idea
of causation is alone derivable from the constant conjunction of objects and the consequent
inference of one from the other ; and, reasoning experimentally, we can only infer from
effects causes exactly adequate to those effects.
But there certainly is a generative power which

is effected by certain instruments: we cannot prove that it is inherent in these instruments; nor is the contrary hypothesis capable of demonstration: we admit that the generative power is incomprehensible; but to suppose that the same effect is produced by an eternal, omniscient, omnipotent being leaves the cause in the same obscurity, but renders it more incomprehensible.

3d, Testimony. It is required that testimony should not be contrary to reason. The testimony that the Deity convinces the senses of men of his existence can only be admitted by us if our mind considers it less probable that these men should have been deceived than that the Deity should have appeared to them. Our reason can never admit the testimony of men, who not only declare that they were eye-witnesses of miracles, but that the Deity was irrational; for he commanded that he should be believed, he proposed the highest rewards for faith, eternal punishments for disbelief. We can only command voluntary actions; belief is not an act of volition; the mind is even passive, or involuntarily active; from this it is evident that we have no sufficient testimony, or rather that testimony is insufficient to prove the being of a God. It has been before shown that it cannot be deduced from reason. They alone, then, who have been convinced by the evidence of the senses can believe it.

Hence it is evident that, having no proofs from either of the three sources of conviction, the mind *cannot* believe the existence of a creative God : it is also evident that, as belief is a passion of the mind, no degree of criminality is attachable to disbelief; and that they only are reprehensible who neglect to remove the false medium through which their mind views any subject of discussion. Every reflecting mind must acknowledge that there is no proof of the existence of a Deity.

God is an hypothesis, and, as such, stands in need of proof: the *onus probandi* rests on the theist. Sir Isaac Newton says : " *Hypotheses non fingo, quicquid enim ex phænomenis non deducitur hypothesis vocanda est, et hypothesis vel metaphysicæ, vel physicæ, vel qualitatum occultarum seu mechanicæ, in philosophiâ locum non habent.*" To all proofs of the existence of a creative God apply this valuable rule. We see a variety of bodies possessing a variety of powers : we merely know their effects ; we are in a state of ignorance with respect to their essences and causes. These Newton calls the phenomena of things ; but the pride of philosophy is unwilling to admit its ignorance of their causes. From the phenomena, which are the objects of our senses, we attempt to infer a cause, which we call God, and gratuitously endow it with all negative and contradictory qualities. From this hypothesis we invent this general name, to conceal our ignorance of causes and essences. The being called God by no means answers with the conditions prescribed by Newton ; it bears every mark of a veil woven by philosophical conceit, to hide the ignorance of philosophers even from themselves. They borrow the threads of its texture from the anthropomorphism of the vulgar. Words have been used by sophists for the same purposes, from the occult qualities of the peripatetics, to the *effluvium* of Boyle and the *crinities* or *nebulæ* of Herschel. God is represented as infinite, eternal, incomprehensible ; he is contained under every predicate in non that the logic of ignorance could fabricate. Even his wor-shippers allow that it is impossible to form any idea of him : they exclaim with the French poet,

" Pour dire ce qu'il est, être lui-même "

Lord Bacon says that atheism leaves to man reason, philosophy, natural piety, laws, repu-tation, and everything that can serve to con-duct him to virtue ; but superstition destroys all these, and erects itself into a tyranny over the misunderstandings of men : hence atheism never disturbs the government, but renders man more clear-sighted, since he sees nothing beyond the boundaries of the present life. — *Bacon's Moral Essays.*

VII. — PAGE 93

Ahasuerus, rise !

" Ahasuerus the Jew crept forth from the dark cave of Mount Carmel. Near two thou-sand years have elapsed since he was first goaded by never-ending restlessness to rove the globe from pole to pole. When our Lord was wearied with the burthen of his ponderous cross, and wanted to rest before the door of Ahasuerus, the unfeeling wretch drove him away with brutality. The Saviour of mankind staggered, sinking under the heavy load, but uttered no complaint. An angel of death appeared before Ahasuerus, and exclaimed indignantly, 'Barbarian! thou hast denied rest to the Son of man: be it denied thee also, until he comes to judge the world.'

"A black demon, let loose from hell upon Ahasuerus, goads him now from country to country; he is denied the consolation which death affords, and precluded from the rest of the peaceful grave.

"Ahasuerus crept forth from the dark cave of Mount Carmel — he shook the dust from his beard — and taking up one of the skulls heaped there, hurled it down the eminence: it rebounded from the earth in shivered atoms. This was my father! roared Ahasuerus. Seven more skulls rolled down from rock to rock; while the infuriate Jew, following them with ghastly looks, exclaimed — And these were my wives! He still continued to hurl down skull after skull, roaring in dreadful accents — And these, and these, and these were my children! They *could die;* but I! reprobate wretch! alas! I cannot die! Dreadful beyond conception is the judgment that hangs over me. Jerusalem fell — I crushed the sucking babe, and precipitated myself into the destructive flames. I cursed the Romans — but, alas! alas! the restless curse held me by the hair, — and I could not die!

"Rome the giantess fell — I placed myself before the falling statue — she fell and did not crush me. Nations sprang up and disappeared before me; — but I remained and did not die. From cloud-encircled cliffs did I precipitate myself into the ocean; but the foaming billows cast me upon the shore, and the burning arrow of existence pierced my cold heart again. I leaped into Etna's flaming abyss, and roared with the giants for ten long months, polluting with my groans the Mount's sulphureous mouth — ah! ten long months. The volcano fermented, and in a fiery stream of lava cast me up. I lay torn by the torture-snakes of hell amid the glowing cinders, and yet continued to exist. — A forest was on fire: I darted on wings of fury and despair

into the crackling wood. Fire dropped upon
me from the trees, but the flames only singed
my limbs; alas! it could not consume them.
—I now mixed with the butchers of mankind,
and plunged in the tempest of the raging
battle. I roared defiance to the infuriate Gaul,
defiance to the victorious German; but arrows
and spears rebounded in shivers from my
body. The Saracen's flaming sword broke
upon my skull: balls in vain hissed upon me:
the lightnings of battle glared harmless around
my loins: in vain did the elephant trample on
me, in vain the iron hoof of the wrathful steed!
The mine, big with destructive power, burst
upon me, and hurled me high in the air—
I fell on heaps of smoking limbs, but was
only singed. The giant's steel club rebounded
from my body; the executioner's hand could
not strangle me, the tiger's tooth could not
pierce me, nor would the hungry lion in the
circus devour me. I cohabited with poisonous
snakes, and pinched the red crest of the
dragon. — The serpent stung, but could not
destroy me. The dragon tormented, but
dared not to devour me. — I now provoked
the fury of tyrants: I said to Nero, Thou art

a bloodhound! I said to Christiern, Thou art a bloodhound! I said to Muley Ismail, Thou art a bloodhound!—The tyrants invented cruel torments, but did not kill me. ... Ha! not to be able to die—not to be able to die—not to be permitted to rest after the toils of life—to be doomed to be imprisoned for ever in the clay-formed dungeon—to be for ever clogged with this worthless body, its load of diseases and infirmities—to be condemned to [be] hold for millenniums that yawning monster Sameness, and Time, that hungry hyena, ever bearing children, and ever devouring again her offspring!—Ha! not to be permitted to die! Awful avenger in heaven, hast thou in thine armory of wrath a punishment more dreadful? then let it thunder upon me, command a hurricane to sweep me down to the foot of Carmel, that I there may lie extended; may pant, and writhe, and die!"

This fragment is the translation of part of some German work, whose title I have vainly endeavoured to discover. I picked it up, dirty and torn, some years ago, in Lincoln's-Inn Fields.

VII. — Page 96

I will beget a son, and he shall bear
The sins of all the world.

A book is put into our hands when children, called the Bible, the purport of whose history is briefly this: That God made the earth in six days, and there planted a delightful garden, in which he placed the first pair of human beings. In the midst of the garden he planted a tree, whose fruit, although within their reach, they were forbidden to touch. That the Devil, in the shape of a snake, persuaded them to eat of this fruit; in consequence of which God condemned both them and their posterity yet unborn to satisfy his justice by their eternal misery. That, four thousand years after these events (the human race in the meanwhile having gone unredeemed to perdition), God engendered with the betrothed wife of a carpenter in Judea (whose virginity was nevertheless uninjured), and begat a son, whose name was Jesus Christ; and who was crucified and died, in order that no more men might be devoted to hell-fire, he bearing the burthen of his Father's displeasure by proxy. The book states, in addition, that the soul of whoever disbelieves this sacrifice will be burned with everlasting fire.

During many ages of misery and darkness this story gained implicit belief; but at length men arose who suspected that it was a fable and imposture, and that Jesus Christ, so far from being a God, was only a man like themselves. But a numerous set of men, who derived and still derive immense emoluments from this opinion, in the shape of a popular belief, told the vulgar that if they did not believe in the Bible they would be damned to all eternity; and burned, imprisoned, and poisoned all the unbiassed and unconnected inquirers who occasionally arose. They still oppress them, so far as the people, now become more enlightened, will allow.

The belief in all that the Bible contains is called Christianity. A Roman governor of Judea, at the instance of a priest-led mob, crucified a man called Jesus eighteen centuries ago. He was a man of pure life, who desired to rescue his countrymen from the tyranny of their barbarous and degrading superstitions. The common fate of all who desire to benefit mankind awaited him. The rabble, at the instigation of the priests, demanded his death, although his very judge made public acknowledgment of his innocence. Jesus was sacrificed to the honour of that God with whom he was afterwards confounded. It is of importance, therefore, to distinguish between the pretended character of this being as the Son of God and the Saviour of the world, and his real character as a man, who, for a vain attempt to reform the world, paid the forfeit of his life to that overbearing tyranny which has since so long desolated the universe in his name. Whilst the one is a hypocritical demon, who announces himself as the God of compassion and peace, even whilst he stretches forth his blood-red hand with the sword of discord to waste the earth, having confessedly devised this scheme of desolation from eternity; the other stands in the foremost list of those true heroes who have died in the glorious martyrdom of liberty, and have braved torture, contempt, and poverty in the cause of suffering humanity.

The vulgar, ever in extremes, became persuaded that the crucifixion of Jesus was a supernatural event. Testimonies of miracles, so frequent in unenlightened ages, were not wanting to prove that he was something divine. This belief, rolling through the lapse of ages, met with the reveries of Plato and the reasonings of Aristotle, and acquired force and extent, until the divinity of Jesus became a dogma, which to dispute was death, which to doubt was infamy.

Christianity is now the established religion: he who attempts to impugn it must be contented to behold murderers and traitors take precedence of him in public opinion; though, if his genius be equal to his courage, and assisted by a peculiar coalition of circumstances, future ages may exalt him to a divinity, and persecute others in his name, as he was persecuted in the name of his predecessor in the homage of the world.

The same means that have supported every other popular belief have supported Christianity. War, imprisonment, assassination, and falsehood: deeds of unexampled and incomparable atrocity have made it what it is. The blood shed by the votaries of the God of mercy and peace, since the establishment of his religion, would probably suffice to drown all other sectaries now on the habitable globe. We derive from our ancestors a faith thus fostered and supported: we quarrel, persecute, and hate for its maintenance Even under a government which, whilst it infringes the very right of thought and speech, boasts of permitting the liberty of the press, a man is pilloried and imprisoned because he is a deist, and no one raises his voice in the indignation of outraged humanity. But it is ever a proof that the falsehood of a proposition is felt by those who use coercion, not reasoning, to procure its admission; and a dispassionate observer would feel himself more powerfully interested in favour of a man who, depending on the truth of his opinions, simply stated his reasons for entertaining them, than in that of his aggressor who, daringly avowing his unwillingness or incapacity to answer them by argument, proceeded to repress the energies and break the spirit of their promulgator by that torture and imprisonment whose infliction he could command.

Analogy seems to favour the opinion that as, like other systems, Christianity has arisen

and augmented, so like them it will decay and
perish; that as violence, darkness, and deceit,
not reasoning and persuasion, have procured
its admission among mankind, so, when enthusiasm has subsided, and time, that infallible
controverter of false opinions, has involved its
pretended evidences in the darkness of antiquity, it will become obsolete; that Milton's
poem alone will give permanency to the re-
membrance of its absurdities; and that men
will laugh as heartily at grace, faith, redemption, and original sin, as they now do at the
metamorphoses of Jupiter, the miracles of
Romish saints, the efficacy of witchcraft, and
the appearance of departed spirits.

Had the Christian religion commenced and
continued by the mere force of reasoning and
persuasion, the preceding analogy would be
inadmissible. We should never speculate on
the future obsoleteness of a system perfectly
conformable to nature and reason: it would
endure so long as they endured; it would be a
truth as indisputable as the light of the sun,
the criminality of murder, and other facts,
whose evidence, depending on our organization
and relative situations, must remain acknowl-

edged as satisfactory so long as man is man. It is an incontrovertible fact, the consideration of which ought to repress the hasty conclusions of credulity, or moderate its obstinacy in maintaining them, that, had the Jews not been a fanatical race of men, had even the resolution of Pontius Pilate been equal to his candour, the Christian religion never could have prevailed, it could not even have existed: on so feeble a thread hangs the most cherished opinion of a sixth of the human race! When will the vulgar learn humility? When will the pride of ignorance blush at having believed before it could comprehend?

Either the Christian religion is true, or it is false: if true, it comes from God, and its authenticity can admit of doubt and dispute no further than its omnipotent author is willing to allow. Either the power or the goodness of God is called in question, if he leaves those doctrines most essential to the well-being of man in doubt and dispute; the only ones which, since their promulgation, have been the subject of unceasing cavil, the cause of irreconcilable hatred. *If God has spoken, why is the universe not convinced?*

Notes to Queen Mab

There is this passage in the Christian Scriptures: "Those who obey not God, and believe not the Gospel of his Son, shall be punished with everlasting destruction." This is the pivot upon which all religions turn: they all assume that it is in our power to believe or not to believe; whereas the mind can only believe that which it thinks true. A human being can only be supposed accountable for those actions which are influenced by his will. But belief is utterly distinct from and unconnected with volition: it is the apprehension of the agreement or disagreement of the ideas that compose any proposition. Belief is a passion, or involuntary operation of the mind, and, like other passions, its intensity is precisely proportionate to the degrees of excitement. Volition is essential to merit or demerit. But the Christian religion attaches the highest possible degrees of merit and demerit to that which is worthy of neither, and which is totally unconnected with the peculiar faculty of the mind, whose presence is essential to their being.

Christianity was intended to reform the world: had an all-wise Being planned it, nothing is more improbable than that it should have failed: omniscience would infallibly have foreseen the inutility of a scheme which experience demonstrates, to this age, to have been utterly unsuccessful.

Christianity inculcates the necessity of supplicating the Deity. Prayer may be considered under two points of view;—as an endeavour to change the intentions of God, or as a formal testimony of our obedience. But the former case supposes that the caprices of a limited intelligence can occasionally instruct the Creator of the world how to regulate the universe; and the latter, a certain degree of servility analogous to the loyalty demanded by earthly tyrants. Obedience indeed is only the pitiful and cowardly egotism of him who thinks that he can do something better than reason.

Christianity, like all other religions, rests upon miracles, prophecies, and martyrdoms. No religion ever existed which had not its prophets, its attested miracles, and, above all, crowds of devotees who would bear patiently the most horrible tortures to prove its authenticity. It should appear that in no case can a discriminating mind subscribe to the genuineness of a miracle. A miracle is an infraction of nature's law, by a supernatural cause; by a cause acting beyond that eternal circle within which all things are included. God breaks through the law of nature, that he may convince mankind of the truth of that revelation which, in spite of his precautions, has been, since its introduction, the subject of unceasing schism and cavil.

Miracles resolve themselves into the following question:[1] — Whether it is more probable the laws of nature, hitherto so immutably harmonious, should have undergone violation, or that a man should have told a lie? Whether it is more probable that we are ignorant of the natural cause of an event, or that we know the supernatural one? That, in old times, when the powers of nature were less known than at present, a certain set of men were themselves deceived, or had some hidden motive for deceiving others; or that God begat a son, who, in his legislation, measuring merit by belief, evidenced himself to be totally ignorant of the powers of the human mind — of what is voluntary, and what is the contrary?

[1] See Hume's " Essay," Vol ii., p. 121.

Notes to Queen Mab

We have many instances of men telling lies; none of an infraction of nature's laws, those laws of whose government alone we have any knowledge or experience. The records of all nations afford innumerable instances of men deceiving others either from vanity or interest or themselves being deceived by the limitedness of their views and their ignorance of natural causes: but where is the accredited case of God having come upon earth, to give the lie to his own creations? There would be something truly wonderful in the appearance of a ghost; but the assertion of a child that he saw one as he passed through the churchyard is universally admitted to be less miraculous.

But even supposing that a man should raise a dead body to life before our eyes, and on this fact rest his claim to being considered the son of God;—the Humane Society restores drowned persons, and because it makes no mystery of the method it employs, its members are not mistaken for the sons of God. All that we have a right to infer from our ignorance of the cause of any event is that we do not know it: had the Mexicans attended to this simple rule when they heard the cannon of the

Spaniards, they would not have considered them as gods: the experiments of modern chemistry would have defied the wisest philosophers of ancient Greece and Rome to have accounted for them on natural principles. An author of strong common sense has observed that "a miracle is no miracle at second-hand;" he might have added that a miracle is no miracle in any case; for until we are acquainted with all natural causes, we have no reason to imagine others.

There remains to be considered another proof of Christianity — prophecy. A book is written before a certain event, in which this event is foretold; how could the prophet have foreknown it without inspiration? how could he have been inspired without God? The greatest stress is laid on the prophecies of Moses and Hosea on the dispersion of the Jews, and that of Isaiah concerning the coming of the Messiah. The prophecy of Moses is a collection of every possible cursing and blessing; and it is so far from being marvellous that the one of dispersion should have been fulfilled, that it would have been more surprising if, out of all these, none should have taken effect. In Deuteronomy, Chap. xxviii. ver. 64, where Moses explicitly foretells the dispersion, he states that they shall there serve gods of wood and stone: " And the Lord shall scatter thee among all people, from the one end of the earth even to the other, *and there thou shalt serve other gods, which neither thou nor thy fathers have known, even gods of wood and stone.*" The Jews are at this day remarkably tenacious of their religion. Moses also declares that they shall be subjected to these curses for disobedience to his ritual: " And it shall come to pass if thou wilt not hearken unto the voice of the Lord thy God, to observe to do all the commandments and statutes which I command you this day, that all these curses shall come upon thee and overtake thee." Is this the real reason? The third, fourth, and fifth chapters of Hosea are a piece of immodest confession. The indelicate type might apply in a hundred senses to a hundred things. The fifty-third chapter of Isaiah is more explicit, yet it does not exceed in clearness the oracles of Delphos. The historical proof that Moses, Isaiah, and Hosea did write when they are said to have written is far from being clear and circumstantial.

Notes to Queen Mab

But prophecy requires proof in its character as a miracle; we have no right to suppose that a man foreknew future events from God, until it is demonstrated that he neither could know them by his own exertions, nor that the writings which contain the prediction could possibly have been fabricated after the event pretended to be foretold. It is more probable that writings, pretending to divine inspiration, should have been fabricated after the fulfilment of their pretended prediction than that they should have really been divinely inspired, when we consider that the latter supposition makes God at once the creator of the human mind and ignorant of its primary powers, particularly as we have numberless instances of false religions, and forged prophecies of things long past, and no accredited case of God having conversed with men directly or indirectly. It is also possible that the description of an event might have foregone its occurrence; but this is far from being a legitimate proof of a divine revelation, as many men, not pretending to the character of a prophet, have nevertheless, in this sense, prophesied.

Notes to Queen Mab

Lord Chesterfield was never yet taken for a prophet, even by a bishop, yet he uttered this remarkable prediction: "The despotic government of France is screwed up to the highest pitch; a revolution is fast approaching; that revolution, I am convinced, will be radical and sanguinary." This appeared in the letters of the prophet long before the accomplishment of this wonderful prediction. Now, have these particulars come to pass, or have they not? If they have, how could the earl have foreknown them without inspiration? If we admit the truth of the Christian religion on testimony such as this, we must admit, on the same strength of evidence, that God has affixed the highest rewards to belief, and the eternal tortures of the never-dying worm to disbelief, both of which have been demonstrated to be involuntary.

The last proof of the Christian religion depends on the influence of the Holy Ghost. Theologians divide the influence of the Holy Ghost into its ordinary and extraordinary modes of operation. The latter is supposed to be that which inspired the prophets and Apostles; and the former to be the Grace of

God, which summarily makes known the truth of his revelation to those whose mind is fitted for its reception by a submissive perusal of his word. Persons convinced in this manner can do anything but account for their conviction, describe the time at which it happened, or the manner in which it came upon them. It is supposed to enter the mind by other channels than those of the senses, and therefore professes to be superior to reason founded on their experience.

Admitting, however, the usefulness or possibility of a divine revelation, unless we demolish the foundations of all human knowledge, it is requisite that our reason should previously demonstrate its genuineness; for, before we extinguish the steady ray of reason and common sense, it is fit that we should discover whether we cannot do without their assistance, whether or no there be any other which may suffice to guide us through the labyrinth of life:[1] for, if a man is to be inspired upon all occasions, if he is to be sure of a thing because he is sure, if the ordinary operations

[1] See Locke's "Essay on the Human Understanding," Book IV, Chap. xix, on Enthusiasm

of the Spirit are not to be considered very extraordinary modes of demonstration, if enthusiasm is to usurp the place of proof, and madness that of sanity, all reasoning is superfluous. The Mahometan dies fighting for his prophet, the Indian immolates himself at the chariot-wheels of Brahma, the Hottentot worships an insect, the Negro a bunch of feathers, the Mexican sacrifices human victims! Their degree of conviction must certainly be very strong: it cannot arise from reasoning, it must from feelings, the reward of their prayers. If each of these should affirm, in opposition to the strongest possible arguments, that inspiration carried internal evidence, I fear their inspired brethren, the orthodox missionaries, would be so uncharitable as to pronounce them obstinate.

Miracles cannot be received as testimonies of a disputed fact, because all human testimony has ever been insufficient to establish the possibility of miracles. That which is incapable of proof itself is no proof of anything else. Prophecy has also been rejected by the test of reason. Those, then, who have been actually inspired are the only true believers in the Christian religion.

VIII. — PAGE 115

Him, still from hope to hope the bliss pursuing,
Which from the exhaustless lore of human weal
Draws on the virtuous mind, the thoughts that rise
In time-destroying infiniteness, gift
With self-enshrined eternity, etc.

Time is our consciousness of the succession of ideas in our mind. Vivid sensation, of either pain or pleasure, makes the time seem long, as the common phrase is, because it renders us more acutely conscious of our ideas. If a mind be conscious of an hundred ideas during one minute, by the clock, and of two hundred during another, the latter of these spaces would actually occupy so much greater extent in the mind as two exceed one in quantity. If, therefore, the human mind, by any future improvement of its sensibility, should become conscious of an infinite number of ideas in a minute, that minute would be eternity. I do not hence infer that the actual space between the birth and death of a man will ever be prolonged ; but that his sensibility

197

is perfectible, and that the number of ideas which his mind is capable of receiving is indefinite. One man is stretched on the rack during twelve hours; another sleeps soundly in his bed: the difference of time perceived by these two persons is immense; one hardly will believe that half an hour has elapsed, the other could credit that centuries had flown during his agony. Thus, the life of a man of virtue and talent, who should die in his thirtieth year, is, with regard to his own feelings, longer than that of a miserable priest-ridden slave, who dreams out a century of dulness. The one has perpetually cultivated his mental faculties, has rendered himself master of his thoughts, can abstract and generalize amid the lethargy of every-day business; — the other can slumber over the brightest moments of his being, and is unable to remember the happiest hour of his life. Perhaps the perishing ephemeron enjoys a longer life than the tortoise.

> " Dark flood of time !
> Roll as it listeth thee — I measure not
> By months or moments thy ambiguous course.
> Another may stand by me on the brink
> And watch the bubble whirled beyond his ken

That pauses at my feet.   The sense of love,
The thirst for action, and the impassioned thought
Prolong my being : if I wake no more,
My life more actual living will contain
Than some gray veterans' of the world's cold school,
Whose listless hours unprofitably roll,
By one enthusiast feeling unredeemed.''

VIII. — PAGE 116

No longer now
He slays the lamb that looks him in the face.

I hold that the depravity of the physical and moral nature of man originated in his unnatural habits of life.   The origin of man, like that of the universe of which he is a part, is enveloped in impenetrable mystery.   His generations either had a beginning, or they had not.   The weight of evidence in favour of each of these suppositions seems tolerably equal; and it is perfectly unimportant to the present argument which is assumed.   The language spoken, however, by the mythology of nearly all religions seems to prove that at some distant period man forsook the path of nature, and sacrificed the purity and happiness of his

being to unnatural appetites.   The date of this
event seems to have also been that of some
great change in the climates of the earth, with
which it has an obvious correspondence.   The
allegory of Adam and Eve eating of the tree
of evil, and entailing upon their posterity the
wrath of God and the loss of everlasting life,
admits of no other explanation than the disease and crime that have flowed from unnatural diet.   Milton was so well aware of this that
he makes Raphael thus exhibit to Adam the
consequence of his disobedience:

> " . . . Immediately a place
> Before his eyes appeared, sad, noisome, dark ;
> A lazar-house it seemed ; wherein were laid
> Numbers of all diseased — all maladies
> Of ghastly spasm, or racking torture, qualms
> Of heart-sick agony, all feverish kinds,
> Convulsions, epilepsies, fierce catarrhs,
> Intestine stone and ulcer, colic pangs,
> Demoniac frenzy, moping melancholy,
> And moon-struck madness, pining atrophy,
> Marasmus, and wide-wasting pestilence,
> Dropsies and asthmas, and joint-racking rheums."

And how many thousands more might not
be added to this frightful catalogue!

Notes to Queen Mab

The story of Prometheus is one likewise which, although universally admitted to be allegorical, has never been satisfactorily explained. Prometheus stole fire from heaven, and was chained for this crime to Mount Caucasus, where a vulture continually devoured his liver, that grew to meet its hunger. Hesiod says that, before the time of Prometheus mankind were exempt from suffering ; that they enjoyed a vigorous youth, and that death, when at length it came, approached like sleep, and gently closed their eyes. Prometheus (who represents the human race) effected some great change in the condition of his nature, and applied fire to culinary purposes ; thus inventing an expedient for screening from his disgust the horrors of the shambles. From this moment his vitals were devoured by the vulture of disease. It consumed his being in every shape of its loathsome and infinite variety, inducing the soul-quelling sinkings of premature and violent death. All vice arose from the ruin of healthful innocence. Tyranny, superstition, commerce, and inequality were then first known, when reason vainly attempted to guide the wanderings of exacerbated passion. I conclude this part of the subject with an extract from Mr. Newton's " Defence of Vegetable Regimen," from whom I have borrowed this interpretation of the fable of Prometheus.

" Making allowance for such transposition of the events of the allegory as time might produce after the important truths were forgotten, which this portion of the ancient mythology was intended to transmit, the drift of the fable seems to be this: Man at his creation was endowed with the gift of perpetual youth; that is, he was not formed to be a sickly suffering creature as we now see him, but to enjoy health, and to sink by slow degrees into the bosom of his parent earth without disease or pain. Prometheus first taught the use of animal food (primus bovem occidit Prometheus [1]) and of fire, with which to render it more digestible and pleasing to the taste. Jupiter, and the rest of the gods, foreseeing the consequences of these inventions, were amused or irritated at the short-sighted devices of the newly-formed creature, and left him to experience the sad effects of them.

[1] Plin. " Nat. Hist." Lib. vii., Sect. 57.

Thirst, the necessary concomitant of a flesh diet" (perhaps of all diet vitiated by culinary preparation), " ensued; water was resorted to, and man forfeited the inestimable gift of health which he had received from heaven : he became diseased, the partaker of a precarious existence, and no longer descended slowly to his grave." [1]

> " But just disease to luxury succeeds,
>   And every death its own avenger breeds ;
>   The fury passions from that blood began,
>   And turned on man a fiercer savage — man "

Man, and the animals whom he has infected with his society, or depraved by his dominion, are alone diseased. The wild hog, the mouflon, the bison, and the wolf, are perfectly exempt from malady, and invariably die either from external violence or natural old age. But the domestic hog, the sheep, the cow, and the dog, are subject to an incredible variety of distempers; and, like the corrupters of their nature, have physicians who thrive upon their miseries. The supereminence of man is like Satan's, a supereminence of pain; and the majority of his species, doomed to penury,

[1] " Return to Nature." Cadell, 1811

disease, and crime, have reason to curse the untoward event that, by enabling him to communicate his sensations, raised him above the level of his fellow animals. But the steps that have been taken are irrevocable. The whole of human science is comprised in one question: How can the advantages of intellect and civilization be reconciled with the liberty and pure pleasures of natural life? How can we take the benefits and reject the evils of the system, which is now interwoven with all the fibres of our being? — I believe that abstinence from animal food and spirituous liquors would in a great measure capacitate us for the solution of this important question.

It is true that mental and bodily derangement is attributable in part to other deviations from rectitude and nature than those which concern diet. The mistakes cherished by society respecting the connection of the sexes, whence the misery and diseases of unsatisfied celibacy, unenjoying prostitution, and the premature arrival of puberty, necessarily spring; the putrid atmosphere of crowded cities; the exhalations of chemical processes; the muffling of our bodies in superfluous apparel; the absurd treatment of infants : — all these and innumerable other causes contribute their mite to the mass of human evil.

Comparative anatomy teaches us that man resembles frugivorous animals in everything, and carnivorous in nothing; he has neither claws wherewith to seize his prey, nor distinct and pointed teeth to tear the living fibre. A mandarin of the first class, with nails two inches long, would probably find them alone inefficient to hold even a hare. After every subterfuge of gluttony, the bull must be degraded into the ox, and the ram into the wether, by an unnatural and inhuman operation, that the flaccid fibre may offer a fainter resistance to rebellious nature. It is only by softening and disguising dead flesh by culinary preparation that it is rendered susceptible of mastication or digestion; and that the sight of its bloody juices and raw horror does not excite intolerable loathing and disgust. Let the advocate of animal food force himself to a decisive experiment on its fitness, and, as Plutarch recommends, tear a living lamb with his teeth, and plunging his head into its vitals slake his thirst with the steaming blood; when fresh from the deed of horror, let him revert to the irresistible instincts of nature that would rise in judgment against it, and say, Nature formed me for such work as this. Then, and then only, would he be consistent.

Man resembles no carnivorous animal. There is no exception, unless man be one, to the rule of herbivorous animals having cellulated colons.

The orang-outang perfectly resembles man both in the order and number of his teeth. The orang-outang is the most anthropomorphous of the ape tribe, all of which are strictly frugivorous. There is no other species of animals, which live on different food, in which this analogy exists. In many frugivorous animals, the canine teeth are more pointed and distinct than those of man. The resemblance also of the human stomach to that of the orang-outang is greater than to that of any other animal.

The intestines are also identical with those of herbivorous animals, which present a larger surface for absorption and have ample and cellulated colons. The cæcum also, though short, is larger than that of carnivorous animals; and even here the orang-outang retains its accustomed similarity.

The structure of the human frame, then, is that of one fitted to a pure vegetable diet, in every essential particular. It is true that the reluctance to abstain from animal food, in those who have been long accustomed to its stimulus, is so great in some persons of weak minds as to be scarcely overcome; but this is far from bringing any argument in its favour. A lamb, which was fed for some time on flesh by a ship's crew, refused its natural diet at the end of the voyage. There are numerous instances of horses, sheep, oxen, and even wood-pigeons, having been taught to live upon flesh, until they have loathed their natural aliment. Young children evidently prefer pastry, oranges, apples, and other fruit, to the flesh of animals; until, by the gradual depravation of the digestive organs, the free use of vegetables has for a time produced serious inconveniences; *for a time*, I say, since there never was an instance wherein a change from spirituous liquors and animal food to vegetables and pure water has failed ultimately to invigorate the body, by rendering its juices bland and consentaneous, and to restore to the mind that cheerfulness and elasticity which not one in fifty possesses on the present system. A love of strong liquors is also with difficulty taught to infants. Almost every one remembers the wry faces which the first glass of port produced. Unsophisticated instinct is invariably unerring; but to decide on the fitness of animal food from the perverted appetites which its constrained adoption produces, is to make the criminal a judge in his own cause: it is even worse, it is appealing to the infatuated drunkard in a question of the salubrity of brandy.

What is the cause of morbid action in the animal system? Not the air we breathe, for our fellow denizens of nature breathe the same uninjured; not the water we drink (if remote from the pollutions of man and his inventions[1]), for the animals drink it, too; not the earth we tread upon; not the unobscured sight

[1] The necessity of resorting to some means of purifying water, and the disease which arises from its adulteration in civilized countries, is sufficiently apparent   See Doctor Lambe's " Reports on Cancer "   I do not assert that the use of water is in itself unnatural, but that the unperverted palate would swallow no liquid capable of occasioning disease

of glorious nature, in the wood, the field, or the expanse of sky and ocean; nothing that we are or do in common with the undiseased inhabitants of the forest. Something, then, wherein we differ from them: our habit of altering our food by fire, so that our appetite is no longer a just criterion for the fitness of its gratification. Except in children, there remain no traces of that instinct which determines, in all other animals, what aliment is natural or otherwise; and so perfectly obliterated are they in the reasoning adults of our species, that it has become necessary to urge considerations drawn from comparative anatomy to prove that we are naturally frugivorous.

Crime is madness. Madness is disease. Whenever the cause of disease shall be discovered, the root, from which all vice and misery have so long overshadowed the globe, will lie bare to the axe. All the exertions of man, from that moment, may be considered as tending to the clear profit of his species. No sane mind in a sane body resolves upon a real crime. It is a man of violent passions, bloodshot eyes, and swollen veins, that alone can grasp the knife of murder. The system of a simple diet promises no Utopian advantages. It is no mere reform of legislation, whilst the furious passions and evil propensities of the human heart, in which it had its origin, are still unassuaged. It strikes at the root of all evil, and is an experiment which may be tried with success, not alone by nations, but by small societies, families, and even individuals. In no cases has a return to vegetable diet produced the slightest injury; in most it has been attended with changes undeniably beneficial. Should ever a physician be born with the genius of Locke, I am persuaded that he might trace all bodily and mental derangements to our unnatural habits, as clearly as that philosopher has traced all knowledge to sensation. What prolific sources of disease are not those mineral and vegetable poisons that have been introduced for its extirpation! How many thousands have become murderers and robbers, bigots and domestic tyrants, dissolute and abandoned adventurers, from the use of fermented liquors; who, had they slaked their thirst only with pure water, would have lived but to diffuse the happiness of their

own unperverted feelings! How many ground-
less opinions and absurd institutions have not
received a general sanction from the sottish-
ness and intemperance of individuals! Who
will assert that, had the populace of Paris sat-
isfied their hunger at the ever-furnished table
of vegetable nature, they would have lent their
brutal suffrage to the proscription-list of Robes-
pierre? Could a set of men, whose passions
were not perverted by unnatural stimuli, look
with coolness on an *auto da fé*? Is it to be
believed that a being of gentle feelings, rising
from his meal of roots, would take delight in
sports of blood? Was Nero a man of tem-
perate life? could you read calm health in his
cheek, flushed with ungovernable propensities
of hatred for the human race? Did Muley
Ismael's pulse beat evenly, was his skin trans-
parent, did his eyes beam with healthfulness
and its invariable concomitants, cheerfulness
and benignity? Though history has decided
none of these questions, a child could not hesitate to answer in the negative. Surely the
bile-suffused cheek of Buonaparte, his wrinkled
brow and yellow eye, the ceaseless inquietude
of his nervous system, speak no less plainly

the character of his unresting ambition than his murders and his victories. It is impossible, had Buonaparte descended from a race of vegetable feeders, that he could have had either the inclination or the power to ascend the throne of the Bourbons. The desire of tyranny could scarcely be excited in the individual, the power to tyrannize would certainly not be delegated by a society neither frenzied by inebriation nor rendered impotent and irrational by disease. Pregnant indeed with inexhaustible calamity is the renunciation of instinct, as it concerns our physical nature; arithmetic cannot enumerate, nor reason perhaps suspect, the multitudinous sources of disease in civilized life. Even common water, that apparently innoxious pabulum, when corrupted by the filth of populous cities, is a deadly and insidious destroyer.[1] Who can wonder that all the inducements held out by God himself in the Bible to virtue should have been vainer than a nurse's tale; and that those dogmas, by which he has there excited ·and justified the most ferocious propensities, should have alone been deemed essential; whilst Christians are

[1] Lambe's " Reports on Cancer "

in the daily practice of all those habits which have infected with disease and crime, not only the reprobate sons, but these favoured children of the common Father's love? Omnipotence itself could not save them from the consequences of this original and universal sin.

There is no disease, bodily or mental, which adoption of vegetable diet and pure water has not infallibly mitigated, wherever the experiment has been fairly tried. Debility is gradually converted into strength; disease into healthfulness; madness, in all its hideous variety, from the ravings of the fettered maniac to the unaccountable irrationalities of ill-temper, that make a hell of domestic life, into a calm and considerate evenness of temper, that alone might offer a certain pledge of the future moral reformation of society. On a natural system of diet, old age would be our last and our only malady; the term of our existence would be protracted; we should enjoy life, and no longer preclude others from the enjoyment of it; all sensational delights would be infinitely more exquisite and perfect; the very sense of being would then be a continued pleasure, such as we now feel it in some few and favoured moments of our youth. By all that is sacred in our hopes for the human race, I conjure those who love happiness and truth to give a fair trial to the vegetable system. Reasoning is surely superfluous on a subject whose merits an experience of six months would set for ever at rest. But it is only among the enlightened and benevolent that so great a sacrifice of appetite and prejudice can be expected, even though its ultimate excellence should not admit of dispute. It is found easier, by the short-sighted victims of disease, to palliate their torments by medicine than to prevent them by regimen. The vulgar of all ranks are invariably sensual and indocile; yet I cannot but feel myself persuaded that when the benefits of vegetable diet are mathematically proved, when it is as clear that those who live naturally are exempt from premature death as that nine is not one, the most sottish of mankind will feel a preference towards a long and tranquil, contrasted with a short and painful life. On the average, out of sixty persons four die in three years. Hopes are entertained that, in April, 1814, a statement will be given that sixty persons, all having lived more than three years on vegetables and pure water, are then *in perfect health.* More than two years have now elapsed; *not one of them has died*; no such example will be found in any sixty persons taken at random. Seventeen persons of all ages (the families of Doctor Lambe and Mr. Newton) have lived for seven years on this diet without a death, and almost without the slightest illness. Surely, when we consider that some of these were infants, and one a martyr to asthma now nearly subdued, we may challenge any seventeen persons taken at random in this city to exhibit a parallel case. Those who may have been excited to question the rectitude of established habits of diet, by these loose remarks, should consult Mr. Newton's luminous and eloquent essay.[1]

When these proofs come fairly before the world, and are clearly seen by all who understand arithmetic, it is scarcely possible that abstinence from aliments demonstrably pernicious should not become universal. In proportion to the number of proselytes, so will be the

[1] "Return to Nature, or Defence of Vegetable Regimen" Cadell, 1811.

weight of evidence; and when a thousand persons can be produced, living on vegetables and distilled water, who have to dread no disease but old age, the world will be compelled to regard animal flesh and fermented liquors as slow but certain poisons. The change which would be produced by simpler habits on political economy is sufficiently remarkable. The monopolizing eater of animal flesh would no longer destroy his constitution by devouring an acre at a meal, and many loaves of bread would cease to contribute to gout, madness and apoplexy, in the shape of a pint of porter, or a dram of gin, when appeasing the long-protracted famine of the hard-working peasant's hungry babes. The quantity of nutritious vegetable matter, consumed in fattening the carcase of an ox, would afford ten times the sustenance, undepraving indeed, and incapable of generating disease, if gathered immediately from the bosom of the earth. The most fertile districts of the habitable globe are now actually cultivated by men for animals, at a delay and waste of aliment absolutely incapable of calculation. It is only the wealthy that can, to any great degree, even now, indulge the unnatural craving for dead flesh, and they pay for the greater license of the privilege by subjection to supernumerary diseases. Again, the spirit of the nation that should take the lead in this great reform would insensibly become agricultural; commerce, with all its vice, selfishness, and corruption, would gradually decline; more natural habits would produce gentler manners, and the excessive complication of political relations would be so far simplified that every individual might feel and understand why he loved his country, and took a personal interest in its welfare. How would England, for example, depend on the caprices of foreign rulers if she contained within herself all the necessaries, and despised whatever they possessed of the luxuries of life? How could they starve her into compliance with their views? Of what consequence would it be that they refused to take her woollen manufactures, when large and fertile tracts of the island ceased to be allotted to the waste of pasturage? On a natural system of diet we should require no spices from India; no wines from Portugal, Spain, France, or Madeira; none of those multitudinous articles of luxury,

for which every corner of the globe is rifled,
and which are the causes of so much individual rivalship, such calamitous and sanguinary
national disputes. In the history of modern
times, the avarice of commercial monopoly, no
less than the ambition of weak and wicked
chiefs, seems to have fomented the universal
discord, to have added stubbornness to the
mistakes of cabinets, and indocility to the in-
fatuation of the people. Let it ever be
remembered that it is the direct influence of
commerce to make the interval between the
richest and the poorest man wider and more
unconquerable. Let it be remembered that it
is a foe to everything of real worth and excellence in the human character. The odious and
disgusting aristocracy of wealth is built upon
the ruins of all that is good in chivalry or
republicanism; and luxury is the forerunner
of a barbarism scarce capable of cure. Is it
impossible to realize a state of society, where
all the energies of man shall be directed to the
protection of his solid happiness? Certainly, if
this advantage (the object of all political speculation) be in any degree attainable, it is attainable only by a community which holds out no

factitious incentives to the avarice and ambition
of the few, and which is internally organized for
the liberty, security, and comfort of the many.
None must be entrusted with power (and
money is the completest species of power) who
do not stand pledged to use it exclusively for
the general benefit. But the use of animal
flesh and fermented liquors directly militates
with this equality of the rights of man. The
peasant cannot gratify these fashionable cravings without leaving his family to starve.
Without disease and war, those sweeping cur-
tailers of population, pasturage would include
a waste too great to be afforded. The labour
requisite to support a family is far lighter[1]
than is usually supposed. The peasantry
work, not only for themselves, but for the
aristocracy, the army, and the manufacturers.

The advantage of a reform in diet is obvi-
ously greater than that of any other. It strikes

[1] It has come under the author's experience that some of the
workmen on an embankment in North Wales, who, in consequence of the inability of the proprietor to pay them, seldom
received their wages, have supported large families by cultivating
small spots of sterile ground by moonlight. In the notes to
Pratt's Poem, "Bread, or the Poor," is an account of an indus-
trious labourer who, by working in a small garden, before and
after his day's task, attained to an enviable state of independence.

at the root of the evil. To remedy the abuses of legislation, before we annihilate the propensities by which they are produced, is to suppose that by taking away the effect the cause will cease to operate. But the efficacy of this system depends entirely on the proselytism of individuals, and grounds its merits, as a benefit to the community, upon the total change of the dietetic habits in its members. It proceeds securely from a number of particular cases to one that is universal, and has this advantage over the contrary mode, that one error does not invalidate all that has gone before.

Let not too much, however, be expected from this system. The healthiest among us is not exempt from hereditary disease. The most symmetrical, athletic, and long-lived is a being inexpressibly inferior to what he would have been, had not the unnatural habits of his ancestors accumulated for him a certain portion of malady and deformity. In the most perfect specimen of civilized man, something is still found wanting by the physiological critic. Can a return to nature, then, instantaneously eradicate predispositions that have been slowly taking root in the silence of innumerable ages? — Indubitably not. All that I contend for is, that from the moment of the relinquishing all unnatural habits no new disease is generated; and that the predisposition to hereditary maladies gradually perishes, for want of its accustomed supply. In cases of consumption, cancer, gout, asthma, and scrofula, such is the invariable tendency of a diet of vegetables and pure water.

Those who may be induced by these remarks to give the vegetable system a fair trial, should, in the first place, date the commencement of their practice from the moment of their conviction. All depends upon breaking through a pernicious habit resolutely and at once. Doctor Trotter [1] asserts that no drunkard was ever reformed by gradually relinquishing his dram. Animal flesh, in its effects on the human stomach, is analogous to a dram. It is similar in the kind, though differing in the degree, of its operation. The proselyte to a pure diet must be warned to expect a temporary diminution of muscular strength. The subtraction of a powerful stimulus will suffice to

[1] See Trotter on the Nervous Temperament.

account for this event. But it is only temporary, and is succeeded by an equable capa-
bility for exertion, far surpassing his former
various and fluctuating strength. Above all,
he will acquire an easiness of breathing, by
which such exertion is performed, with a
remarkable exemption from that painful and
difficult panting now felt by almost every one
after hastily climbing an ordinary mountain.
He will be equally capable of bodily exertion,
or mental application, after as before his simple
meal. He will feel none of the narcotic effects
of ordinary diet. Irritability, the direct consequence of exhausting stimuli, would yield to
the power of natural and tranquil impulses.
He will no longer pine under the lethargy of
ennui, that unconquerable weariness of life,
more to be dreaded than death itself. He will
escape the epidemic madness, which broods
over its own injurious notions of the Deity,
and " realizes the hell that priests and beldams
feign." Every man forms, as it were, his god
from his own character; to the divinity of one
of simple habits no offering would be more
acceptable than the happiness of his creatures.
He would be incapable of hating or persecuting

others for the love of God. He will find, moreover, a system of simple diet to be a system of perfect epicurism. He will no longer be incessantly occupied in blunting and destroying those organs from which he expects his gratification. The pleasures of taste to be derived from a dinner of potatoes, beans, peas, turnips, lettuces, with a dessert of apples, gooseberries, strawberries, currants, raspberries, and in winter, oranges, apples, and pears, is far greater than is supposed. Those who wait until they can eat this plain fare with the sauce of appetite will scarcely join with the hypocritical sensualist at a lord mayor's feast, who declaims against the pleasures of the table. Solomon kept a thousand concubines, and owned in despair that all was vanity. The man whose happiness is constituted by the society of one amiable woman would find some difficulty in sympathizing with the disappointment of this venerable debauchee.

I address myself not only to the young enthusiast, the ardent devotee of truth and virtue, the pure and passionate moralist, yet unvitiated by the contagion of the world. He will embrace a pure system, from its abstract truth, its beauty, its simplicity, and its promise of wide-extended benefit; unless custom has turned poison into food, he will hate the brutal pleasures of the chase by instinct; it will be a contemplation full of horror and disappointment to his mind, that beings capable of the gentlest and most admirable sympathies should take delight in the death-pangs and last convulsions of dying animals. The elderly man, whose youth has been poisoned by intemperance, or who has lived with apparent moderation, and is afflicted with a variety of painful maladies, would find his account in a beneficial change produced without the risk of poisonous medicines. The mother, to whom the perpetual restlessness of disease and unaccountable deaths incident to her children are the causes of incurable unhappiness, would on this diet experience the satisfaction of beholding their perpetual healths and natural playfulness.[1]

[1] See Mr. Newton's book. His children are the most beautiful and healthy creatures it is possible to conceive; the girls are perfect models for a sculptor; their dispositions are also the most gentle and conciliating; the judicious treatment, which they experience in other points, may be a correlative cause of this. In the first five years of their life, of eighteen thousand children that are born, 7,500 die of various diseases; and how many more of those that survive are not rendered

The most valuable lives are daily destroyed by diseases that it is dangerous to palliate and impossible to cure by medicine. How much longer will man continue to pimp for the gluttony of Death, his most insidious, implacable, and eternal foe?

miserable by maladies not immediately mortal? The quality and quantity of a woman's milk are materially injured by the use of dead flesh. In an island near Iceland, where no vegetables are to be got, the children invariably die of tetanus before they are three weeks old, and the population is supplied from the mainland. — *Sir G. Mackenzie's Hist. of Iceland.* See also " Emile," Chap. i. pp, 53, 54, 56.

Note on Queen Mab, by Mrs. Shelley

SHELLEY was eighteen when he wrote "Queen Mab;" he never published it. When it was written, he had come to the decision that he was too young to be a "judge of controversies;" and he was desirous of acquiring "that sobriety of spirit which is the characteristic of true heroism." But he never doubted the truth or utility of his opinions; and, in printing and privately distributing "Queen Mab," he believed that he should further their dissemination, without occasioning the mischief either to others or himself that might arise from publication. It is doubtful whether he would himself have

admitted it into a collection of his works,
His severe classical taste, refined by the constant study of the Greek poets, might have
discovered defects that escape the ordinary
reader; and the change his opinions underwent
in many points would have prevented him
from putting forth the speculations of his
boyish days. But the poem is too beautiful
in itself, and far too remarkable as the production of a boy of eighteen, to allow of its
being passed over: besides that, having been
frequently reprinted, the omission would be
vain. In the former edition certain portions
were left out, as shocking the general reader
from the violence of their attack on religion.
I myself had a painful feeling that such erasures
might be looked upon as a mark of disrespect
toward the author, and am glad to have the
opportunity of restoring them. The notes
also are reprinted entire — not because they
are models of reasoning or lessons of truth,
but because Shelley wrote them, and that all
that a man at once so distinguished and so
excellent ever did deserves to be preserved.
The alterations his opinions underwent ought
to be recorded, for they form his history.

Notes to Queen Mab

A series of articles was published in the *New Monthly Magazine* during the autumn of the year 1832, written by a man of great talent, a fellow collegian and warm friend of Shelley : they describe admirably the state of his mind during his collegiate life. Inspired with ardour for the acquisition of knowledge, endowed with the keenest sensibility and with the fortitude of a martyr, Shelley came among his fellow creatures, congregated for the purposes of education, like a spirit from another sphere ; too delicately organized for the rough treatment man uses toward man, especially in the season of youth, and too resolute in carrying out his own sense of good and justice, not to become a victim. To a devoted attachment to those he loved he added a determined resistance to oppression. Refusing to fag at Eton, he was treated with revolting cruelty by masters and boys : this roused instead of taming his spirit, and he rejected the duty of obedience when it was enforced by menaces and punishment. To aversion to the society of his fellow creatures, such as he found them when collected together in societies, where one egged on the other to acts of tyranny, was joined the deepest

sympathy and compassion; while the attachment he felt for individuals, and the admiration
with which he regarded their powers and their
virtues, led him to entertain a high opinion of
the perfectibility of human nature; and he believed that all could reach the highest grade of
moral improvement, did not the customs and
prejudices of society foster evil passions and
excuse evil actions.

The oppression which, trembling at every
nerve yet resolute to heroism, it was his ill-
fortune to encounter at school and at college,
led him to dissent in all things from those
whose arguments were blows, whose faith appeared to engender blame and hatred. " During my existence," he wrote to a friend in
1812, " I have incessantly speculated, thought,
and read." His readings were not always well
chosen; among them were the works of the
French philosophers: as far as metaphysical
argument went, he temporarily became a con-
vert. At the same time, it was the cardinal
article of his faith that, if men were but taught
and induced to treat their fellows with love,
charity, and equal rights, this earth would
realize paradise. He looked upon religion, as

it is professed, and above all practised, as hostile instead of friendly to the cultivation of those virtues which would make men brothers.

Can this be wondered at? At the age of seventeen, fragile in health and frame, of the purest habits in morals, full of devoted generosity and universal kindness, glowing with ardour to attain wisdom, resolved at every personal sacrifice to do right, burning with a desire for affection and sympathy, — he was treated as a reprobate, cast forth as a criminal.

The cause was that he was sincere; that he believed the opinions which he entertained to be true. And he loved truth with a martyr's love; he was ready to sacrifice station and fortune, and his dearest affections, at its shrine. The sacrifice was demanded from, and made by, a youth of seventeen. It is a singular fact in the history of society in the civilized nations of modern times that no false step is so irretrievable as one made in early youth. Older men, it is true, when they oppose their fellows and transgress ordinary rules, carry a certain prudence or hypocrisy as a shield along with them. But youth is rash; nor can it imagine, while asserting what it believes to be true, and doing what it believes to be right, that it should be denounced as vicious, and pursued as a criminal.

Shelley possessed a quality of mind which experience has shown me to be of the rarest occurrence among human beings: this was his *unworldliness*. The usual motives that rule men, prospects of present or future advantage, the rank and fortune of those around, the taunts and censures, or the praise, of those who were hostile to him, had no influence whatever over his actions, and apparently none over his thoughts. It is difficult even to express the simplicity and directness of purpose that adorned him. Some few might be found in the history of mankind, and some one at least among his own friends, equally disinterested and scornful, even to severe personal sacrifices, of every baser motive. But no one, I believe, ever joined this noble but passive virtue to equal active endeavours for the benefit of his friends and mankind in general, and to equal power to produce the advantages he desired. The world's brightest gauds and its most solid advantages were of no worth in his eyes, when compared to the cause of what he considered truth, and the good of his fellow creatures. Born in a position which, to his inexperienced mind, afforded the greatest facilities to practise the tenets he espoused, he boldly declared the use he would make of fortune and station, and enjoyed the belief that he should materially benefit his fellow creatures by his actions ; while, conscious of surpassing powers of reason and imagination, it is not strange that he should, even while so young, have believed that his written thoughts would tend to disseminate opinions which he believed conducive to the happiness of the human race.

If man were a creature devoid of passion, he might have said and done all this with quietness. But he was too enthusiastic, and too full of hatred of all the ills he witnessed, not to scorn danger. Various disappointments tortured, but could not tame, his soul. The more enmity he met, the more earnestly he became attached to his peculiar views, and hostile to those of the men who persecuted him.

He was animated to greater zeal by compassion for his fellow creatures. His sympathy was excited by the misery with which the world is burning. He witnessed the sufferings of the poor, and was aware of the evils of ignorance. He desired to induce every rich man to despoil himself of superfluity, and to create a brotherhood of property and service, and was ready to be the first to lay down the advantages of his birth. He was of too uncompromising a disposition to join any party. He did not in his youth look forward to gradual improvement: nay, in those days of intolerance, now almost forgotten, it seemed as easy to look forward to the sort of millennium of freedom and brotherhood which he thought the proper state of mankind as to the present reign of moderation and improvement. Ill-health made him believe that his race would soon be run; that a year or two was all he had of life. He desired that these years should be useful and illustrious. He saw, in a fervent call on his fellow creatures to share alike the blessings of the creation, to love and serve each other, the noblest work that life and time permitted him. In this spirit he composed "Queen Mab."

He was a lover of the wonderful and wild

in literature, but had not fostered these tastes at their genuine sources — the romances and chivalry of the middle ages — but in the perusal of such German works as were current in those days. Under the influence of these he, at the age of fifteen, wrote two short prose romances of slender merit. The sentiments and language were exaggerated, the composition imitative and poor. He wrote also a poem on the subject of Ahasuerus — being led to it by a German fragment he picked up, dirty and torn, in Lincoln's Inn Fields. This fell afterwards into other hands, and was considerably altered before it was printed. Our earlier English poetry was almost unknown to him. The love and knowledge of nature developed by Wordsworth — the lofty melody and mysterious beauty of Coleridge's poetry — and the wild fantastic machinery and gorgeous scenery adopted by Southey — composed his favourite reading; the rhythm of "Queen Mab" was founded on that of "Thalaba," and the first few lines bear a striking resemblance in spirit, though not in idea, to the opening of that poem. His fertile imagination, and ear tuned to the finest sense of harmony,

Notes to Queen Mab

preserved him from imitation. Another of his favourite books was the poem of "Gebir" by Walter Savage Landor. From his boyhood he had a wonderful facility of versification, which he carried into another language; and his Latin school-verses were composed with an ease and correctness that procured for him prizes, and caused him to be resorted to by all his friends for help. He was, at the period of writing "Queen Mab," a great traveller within the limits of England, Scotland, and Ireland. His time was spent among the loveliest scenes of these countries. Mountain and lake and forest were his home; the phenomena of nature were his favourite study. He loved to inquire into their causes, and was addicted to pursuits of natural philosophy and chemistry, as far as they could be carried on as an amusement. These tastes gave truth and vivacity to his descriptions, and warmed his soul with that deep admiration for the wonders of nature which constant association with her inspired.

He never intended to publish "Queen Mab" as it stands; but a few years after, when printing "Alastor," he extracted a small portion which he entitled " The Dæmon of the World." In this he changed somewhat the versification, and made other alterations scarcely to be called improvements.

Some years after, when in Italy, a bookseller published an edition of " Queen Mab" as it originally stood. Shelley was hastily written to by his friends, under the idea that, deeply injurious as the mere distribution of the poem had proved, the publication might awaken fresh persecutions. At the suggestion of these friends he wrote a letter on the subject, printed in the *Examiner* newspaper — with which I close this history of his earliest work.

To the Editor of the Examiner.

" SIR : — Having heard that a poem entitled ' Queen Mab' has been surreptitiously published in London, and that legal proceedings have been instituted against the publisher, I request the favour of your insertion of the following explanation of the affair, as it relates to me.

" A poem entitled ' Queen Mab' was written by me at the age of eighteen, I daresay in a sufficiently intemperate spirit — but even then was not intended for publication, and a few copies only were struck off, to be distributed among my personal friends. I have not seen this production for several years. I doubt not but that it is perfectly worthless in point of literary composition; and that, in all that concerns moral and political speculation, as well as in the subtler discriminations of metaphysical and religious doctrine, it is still more crude and immature. I am a devoted enemy to religious, political, and domestic oppression; and I regret this publication, not so much from literary vanity, as because I fear it is better fitted to injure than to serve the sacred cause of freedom. I have directed my solicitor to apply to Chancery for an injunction to restrain the sale; but, after the precedent of Mr. Southey's 'Wat Tyler' (a poem written, I believe, at the same age, and with the same unreflecting enthusiasm), with little hope of success.

"Whilst I exonerate myself from all share in having divulged opinions hostile to existing sanctions, under the form, whatever it may be, which they assume in this poem, it is scarcely necessary for me to protest against the system of inculcating the truth of Christianity or the excellence of monarchy, however true or however excellent they may be, by such equivocal arguments as confiscation and imprisonment, and invective and slander, and the insolent violation of the most sacred ties of nature and society.

" Sir, I am your obliged and obedient servant,

" Percy B. Shelley.

" Pisa, *June 22, 1821.*"

The Dæmon of the World

A Fragment[1]

[1] A fragment of " Queen Mab " revised

The Dæmon of the World

Part I.

Nec tantum prodere vati,
Quantum scire licet.   Venit ætas omnis in unam
Congeriem, miserumque premunt tot sæcula pectus.
Lucan, Phars. L. v. l. 176.

HOW wonderful is Death,
    Death and his brother Sleep!
    One pale as yonder wan and
        hornèd moon,
  With lips of lurid blue,
The other glowing like the vital morn,
  When throned on ocean's wave
  It breathes over the world:
Yet both so passing strange and wonderful!

The Dæmon of the World

Hath then the iron-sceptred Skeleton,
Whose reign is in the tainted sepulchres,
To the hell dogs that couch beneath his
    throne
Cast that fair prey?   Must that divinest
    form,
Which love and admiration cannot view
Without a beating heart, whose azure veins
Steal like dark streams along a field of
    snow,
Whose outline is as fair as marble clothed
In light of some sublimest mind, decay?
      Nor putrefaction's breath
Leave aught of this pure spectacle
      But loathsomeness and ruin? —
      Spare aught but a dark theme,
On which the lightest heart might moral-
    ize?
Or is it but that downy-wingèd slumbers
Have charmed their nurse coy Silence near her
      lids
      To watch their own repose?
      Will they, when morning's beam

The Dæmon of the World

Flows through those wells of light,
Seek far from noise and day some western
    cave,
Where woods and streams with soft and paus-
    ing winds
    A lulling murmur weave? —

    Ianthe doth not sleep
    The dreamless sleep of death :
Nor in her moonlight chamber silently
Doth Henry hear her regular pulses throb,
    Or mark her delicate cheek
With interchange of hues mock the broad
    moon,
    Outwatching weary night,
    Without assured reward.
    Her dewy eyes are closed;
On their translucent lids, whose texture fine
Scarce hides the dark blue orbs that burn
    below
    With unapparent fire,
    The baby Sleep is pillowed :
    Her golden tresses shade

The Dæmon of the World

The bosom's stainless pride,
Twining like tendrils of the parasite
    Around a marble column.

    Hark! whence that rushing sound?
    'Tis like a wondrous strain that sweeps
    Around a lonely ruin
When west winds sigh and evening waves
        respond
    In whispers from the shore:
'Tis wilder than the unmeasured notes
Which from the unseen lyres of dells and
        groves
    The genii of the breezes sweep.
Floating on waves of music and of light
The chariot of the Dæmon of the World
    Descends in silent power:
Its shape reposed within: slight as some
        cloud
That catches but the palest tinge of day
    When evening yields to night,
Bright as that fibrous woof when stars indue
    Its transitory robe.

244

The Dæmon of the World

Four shapeless shadows bright and beautiful
Draw that strange car of glory, reins of light
Check their unearthly speed; they stop and
    fold
      Their wings of braided air :
The Dæmon leaning from the ethereal car
      Gazed on the slumbering maid.
Human eye hath ne'er beheld
A shape so wild, so bright, so beautiful,
As that which o'er the maiden's charmèd sleep,
      Waving a starry wand,
      Hung like a mist of light.
Such sounds as breathed around like odorous
      winds
      Of wakening spring arose,
Filling the chamber and the moonlight sky.

Maiden, the world's supremest spirit
      Beneath the shadow of her wings
Folds all thy memory doth inherit
      From ruin of divinest things,
        Feelings that lure thee to betray,
        And light of thoughts that pass away.

The Dæmon of the World

For thou hast earned a mighty boon,
    The truths which wisest poets see
Dimly, thy mind may make its own,
    Rewarding its own majesty,
        Entranced in some diviner mood
        Of self-oblivious solitude.

Custom, and Faith, and Power thou spurnest;
    From hate and awe thy heart is free;
Ardent and pure as day thou burnest,
    For dark and cold mortality
        A living light, to cheer it long,
        The watch-fires of the world among.

Therefore from nature's inner shrine,
    Where gods and fiends in worship bend,
Majestic spirit, be it thine
    The flame to seize, the veil to rend,
        Where the vast snake Eternity
        In charmèd sleep doth ever lie.

All that inspires thy voice of love,
    Or speaks in thy unclosing eyes,

The Dæmon of the World

Or through thy frame doth burn or move,
  Or think or feel, awake, arise!
    Spirit, leave for mine and me
    Earth's unsubstantial mimicry!

It ceased, and from the mute and moveless
    frame
  A radiant spirit arose,
All beautiful in naked purity.
Robed in its human hues it did ascend,
Disparting as it went the silver clouds
It moved towards the car, and took its seat
  Beside the Dæmon shape.

Obedient to the sweep of aery song,
  The mighty ministers
Unfurled their prismy wings.
  The magic car moved on;
The night was fair, innumerable stars
  Studded heaven's dark blue vault;
  The eastern wave grew pale
  With the first smile of morn.

The Dæmon of the World

The magic car moved on.
From the swift sweep of wings
The atmosphere in flaming sparkles flew;
And where the burning wheels
Eddied above the mountain's loftiest peak
Was traced a line of lightning.
Now far above a rock the utmost verge
Of the wide earth it flew,
The rival of the Andes, whose dark brow
Frowned o'er the silver sea.

Far, far below the chariot's stormy path,
Calm as a slumbering babe,
Tremendous ocean lay.
Its broad and silent mirror gave to view
The pale and waning stars,
The chariot's fiery track,
And the gray light of morn
Tingeing those fleecy clouds
That cradled in their folds the infant dawn.
The chariot seemed to fly
Through the abyss of an immense concave,
Radiant with million constellations, tinged

248

The Dæmon of the World

With shades of infinite colour,
And semicircled with a belt
Flashing incessant meteors.

As they approached their goal,
The wingèd shadows seemed to gather speed.
The sea no longer was distinguished; earth
Appeared a vast and shadowy sphere, suspended
    In the black concave of heaven
    With the sun's cloudless orb,
    Whose rays of rapid light
Parted around the chariot's swifter course,
And fell like ocean's feathery spray
    Dashed from the boiling surge
    Before a vessel's prow.

    The magic car moved on.
    Earth's distant orb appeared
The smallest light that twinkles in the heavens,
    Whilst round the chariot's way
Innumerable systems widely rolled,
    And countless spheres diffused
      An ever varying glory.

249

The Dæmon of the World

It was a sight of wonder! Some were horned,
And, like the moon's argentine crescent hung
In the dark dome of heaven, some did shed
A clear mild beam like Hesperus, while the
     sea
Yet glows with fading sunlight; others dashed
Athwart the night with trains of bickering
     fire,
Like spherèd worlds to death and ruin driven;
Some shone like stars, and as the chariot passed
     Bedimmed all other light.

     Spirit of Nature! here
In this interminable wilderness
Of worlds, at whose involved immensity
     Even soaring fancy staggers,
     Here is thy fitting temple.
     Yet not the lightest leaf
That quivers to the passing breeze
     Is less instinct with thee, —
     Yet not the meanest worm,
That lurks in graves and fattens on the dead
     Less shares thy eternal breath.

250

The Dæmon of the World

Spirit of Nature! thou
Imperishable as this glorious scene,
    Here is thy fitting temple.

If solitude hath ever led thy steps
To the shore of the immeasurable sea,
    And thou hast lingered there
    Until the sun's broad orb
Seemed resting on the fiery line of ocean,
Thou must have marked the braided webs of
      gold
    That without motion hang
    Over the sinking sphere.
Thou must have marked the billowy mountain
      clouds,
Edged with intolerable radiancy,
    Towering like rocks of jet
    Above the burning deep:
    And yet there is a moment
    When the sun's highest point
Peers like a star o'er ocean's western edge,
When those far clouds of feathery purple gleam
Like fairy lands girt by some heavenly sea:

The Dæmon of the World

Then has thy rapt imagination soared
Where in the midst of all existing things
The temple of the mightiest Dæmon stands.

Yet not the golden islands
That gleam amid yon flood of purple light,
    Nor the feathery curtains
That canopy the sun's resplendent couch,
    Nor the burnished ocean waves
    Paving that gorgeous dome,
    So fair, so wonderful a sight
As the eternal temple could afford.
The elements of all that human thought
Can frame of lovely or sublime, did join
To rear the fabric of the fane, nor aught
Of earth may image forth its majesty.
Yet likest evening's vault that faëry hall,
As   heaven   low   resting   on   the   wave   it
        spread
    Its floors of flashing light,
    Its vast and azure dome;
And on the verge of that obscure abyss
Where crystal battlements o'erhang the gulph

The Dæmon of the World

Of the dark world, ten thousand spheres diffuse
Their lustre through its adamantine gates.

    The magic car no longer moved;
    The Dæmon and the Spirit
    Entered the eternal gates.
    Those clouds of aery gold
    That slept in glittering billows
    Beneath the azure canopy,
With the ethereal footsteps trembled not;
    While slight and odorous mists
Floated to strains of thrilling melody
Through the vast columns and the pearly
      shrines.

    The Dæmon and the Spirit
Approached the overhanging battlement.
Below lay stretched the boundless universe!
    There, far as the remotest line
That limits swift imagination's flight,
Unending orbs mingled in mazy motion,
    Immutably fulfilling
    Eternal Nature's law.

The Dæmon of the World

Above, below, around,
The circling systems formed
A wilderness of harmony,
Each with undeviating aim
In eloquent silence through the depths of space
   Pursued its wondrous way. —

Awhile the Spirit paused in ecstasy.
Yet soon she saw, as the vast spheres swept by,
Strange things within their belted orbs appear.
Like animated frenzies, dimly moved
Shadows, and skeletons, and fiendly shapes,
Thronging round human graves, and o'er the
      dead
Sculpturing records for each memory
In verse, such as malignant gods pronounce,
Blasting the hopes of men, when heaven and
      hell
Confounded burst in ruin o'er the world:
And they did build vast trophies, instruments
Of murder, human bones, barbaric gold,
Skins torn from living men, and towers of
      skulls

The Dæmon of the World

With sightless holes gazing on blinder heaven,
Mitres, and crowns, and brazen chariots stained
With blood, and scrolls of mystic wickedness,
The sanguine codes of venerable crime.
The likeness of a thronèd king came by,
When these had past, bearing upon his brow
A threefold crown; his countenance was calm,
His eye severe and cold; but his right hand
Was charged with bloody coin, and he did
    gnaw
By fits, with secret smiles, a human heart
Concealed beneath his robe; and motley
    shapes,
A multitudinous throng, around him knelt,
With bosoms bare, and bowed heads, and false
    looks
Of true submission, as the sphere rolled by,
Brooking no eye to witness their foul shame,
Which human hearts must feel, while human
    tongues
Tremble to speak, they did rage horribly,
Breathing in self contempt fierce blasphemies
Against the Dæmon of the World, and high

The Dæmon of the World

Hurling their armèd hands where the pure
    Spirit,
Serene and inaccessibly secure,
Stood on an isolated pinnacle,
The flood of ages combating below
The depth of the unbounded universe
    Above, and all around
Necessity's unchanging harmony.

Part II.

HAPPY Earth! reality of
   Heaven!
To which those restless powers
   that ceaselessly
Throng through the human universe, aspire;
Thou consummation of all mortal hope!
Thou glorious prize of blindly working will!
Whose rays, diffused throughout all space and
   time,
Verge to one point and blend for ever there:
Of purest spirits thou pure dwelling-place!
Where care and sorrow, impotence and crime,
Languor, disease, and ignorance dare not
   come:
O happy Earth! reality of Heaven!

  Genius has seen thee in her passionate
   dreams,
And dim forebodings of thy loveliness

The Dæmon of the World

Haunting the human heart, have there en-
 twined
Those rooted hopes, that the proud Power
 of Evil
Shall not for ever on this fairest world
Shake pestilence and war, or that his slaves
With blasphemy for prayer, and human blood
For sacrifice, before his shrine for ever
In adoration bend, or Erebus
With all its banded fiends shall not uprise
To overwhelm in envy and revenge
The dauntless and the good, who dare to
 hurl
Defiance at his throne, girt tho' it be
With Death's omnipotence. Thou hast be-
 held
His empire, o'er the present and the past;
It was a desolate sight — now gaze on mine,
Futurity. Thou hoary giant Time,
Render thou up thy half-devoured babes, —
And from the cradles of eternity,
Where millions lie lulled to their portioned
 sleep

The Dæmon of the World

By the deep murmuring stream of passing
    things,
Tear thou that gloomy shroud. — Spirit, be-
    hold
Thy glorious destiny !

               The Spirit saw
The vast frame of the renovated world
Smile in the lap of Chaos, and the sense
Of hope thro' her fine texture did suffuse
Such varying glow, as summer evening casts
On undulating clouds and deepening lakes.
Like the vague sighings of a wind at even,
That wakes the wavelets of the slumbering sea
And dies on the creation of its breath,
And sinks and rises, fails and swells by fits,
Was the sweet stream of thought that with
    wild motion
Flowed o'er the Spirit's human sympathies.
The mighty tide of thought had paused awhile,
Which from the Dæmon now like Ocean's
    stream
Again began to pour. —

The Dæmon of the World

To me is given
The wonders of the human world to keep —
Space, matter, time and mind — let the sight
Renew and strengthen all thy failing hope.
All things are recreated, and the flame
Of consentaneous love inspires all life:
The fertile bosom of the earth gives suck
To myriads, who still grow beneath her care,
Rewarding her with their pure perfectness:
The balmy breathings of the wind inhale
Her virtues, and diffuse them all abroad:
Health floats amid the gentle atmosphere,
Glows in the fruits, and mantles on the
    stream:
No storms deform the beaming brow of
    heaven,
Nor scatter in the freshness of its pride
The foliage of the undecaying trees;
But fruits are ever ripe, flowers ever fair,
And Autumn proudly bears her matron grace,
Kindling a flush on the fair cheek of Spring,
Whose virgin bloom beneath the ruddy fruit
Reflects its tint and blushes into love.

The Dæmon of the World

The habitable earth is full of bliss;
Those wastes of frozen billows that were
    hurled
By everlasting snow-storms round the poles,
Where matter dared not vegetate nor live,
But ceaseless frost round the vast solitude
Bound its broad zone of stillness, are un-
    loosed;
And fragrant zephyrs there from spicy isles
Ruffle the placid ocean-deep, that rolls
Its broad, bright surges to the sloping sand,
Whose roar is wakened into echoings sweet
To murmur through the heaven-breathing
    groves
And melodize with man's blest nature there.

The vast tract of the parched and sandy
    waste
Now teems with countless rills and shady
    woods,
Corn-fields and pastures and white cottages;
And where the startled wilderness did hear
A savage conqueror stained in kindred blood,

The Dæmon of the World

Hymning his victory, or the milder snake
Crushing the bones of some frail antelope
Within his brazen folds — the dewy lawn,
Offering sweet incense to the sunrise, smiles
To see a babe before his mother's door,
Share with the green and golden basilisk
That comes to lick his feet, his morning's
    meal.

  Those trackless deeps, where many a weary
    sail
Has seen above the illimitable plain,
Morning on night, and night on morning rise,
Whilst still no land to greet the wanderer
    spread
Its shadowy mountains on the sun-bright sea,
Where the loud roarings of the tempest-waves
So long have mingled with the gusty wind
In melancholy loneliness, and swept
The desert of those ocean solitudes,
But vocal to the sea-bird's harrowing shriek,
The bellowing monster, and the rushing storm,
Now to the sweet and many-mingling sounds

The Dæmon of the World

Of kindliest human impulses respond:
Those lonely realms bright garden-isles begem,
With lightsome clouds and shining seas be-
    tween,
And fertile valleys, resonant with bliss,
Whilst green woods overcanopy the wave,
Which like a toil-worn labourer leaps to shore,
To meet the kisses of the flowerets there.

  Man chief perceives the change, his being
    notes
The gradual renovation, and defines
Each movement of its progress on his mind.
Man, where the gloom of the long polar night
Lowered o'er the snow-clad rocks and frozen
    soil,
Where scarce the hardest herb that braves the
    frost
Basked in the moonlight's ineffectual glow,
Shrank with the plants, and darkened with the
    night;
Nor where the tropics bound the realms of day
With a broad belt of mingling cloud and flame,

The Dæmon of the World

Where blue mists through the unmoving atmos-
    phere
Scattered the seeds of pestilence, and fed
Unnatural vegetation, where the land
Teemed with all earthquake, tempest and dis-
    ease,
Was man a nobler being; slavery
Had crushed him to his country's blood-stained
    dust.

Even where the milder zone afforded man
A seeming shelter, yet contagion there,
Blighting his being with unnumbered ills,
Spread like a quenchless fire; nor truth availed
Till late to arrest its progress, or create
That peace which first in bloodless victory
    waved
Her snowy standard o'er this favoured clime:
There man was long the train-bearer of
    slaves,
The mimic of surrounding misery,
The jackal of ambition's lion-rage,
The bloodhound of religion's hungry zeal.

The Dæmon of the World

Here now the human being stands adorning
This loveliest earth with taintless body and
    mind;
Blest from his birth with all bland impulses,
Which gently in his noble bosom wake
All kindly passions and all pure desires.
Him, still from hope to hope the bliss pursu-
    ing,
Which from the exhaustless lore of human weal
Draws on the virtuous mind, the thoughts that
    rise
In time-destroying infiniteness, gift
With self-enshrined eternity, that mocks
The unprevailing hoariness of age,
And man, once fleeting o'er the transient scene
Swift as an unremembered vision, stands
Immortal upon earth: no longer now
He slays the beast that sports around his dwell-
    ing
And horribly devours its mangled flesh,
Or drinks its vital blood, which like a stream
Of poison thro' his fevered veins did flow
Feeding a plague that secretly consumed

The Dæmon of the World

His feeble frame, and kindling in his mind
Hatred, despair, and fear and vain belief,
The germs of misery, death, disease, and crime.
No longer now the wingèd habitants,
That in the woods their sweet lives sing away,
Flee from the form of man ; but gather round,
And prune their sunny feathers on the hands
Which little children stretch in friendly sport
Towards these dreadless partners of their play.
All things are void of terror : man has lost
His desolating privilege, and stands
An equal amidst equals : happiness
And science dawn though late upon the earth ;
Peace cheers the mind, health renovates the
        frame ;
Disease and pleasure cease to mingle here,
Reason and passion cease to combat there ;
Whilst mind unfettered o'er the earth extends
Its all-subduing energies, and wields
The sceptre of a vast dominion there.

Mild is the slow necessity of death :
The tranquil spirit fails beneath its grasp,

The Dæmon of the World

Without a groan, almost without a fear,
Resigned in peace to the necessity,
Calm as a voyager to some distant land,
And full of wonder, full of hope as he.
The deadly germs of languor and disease
Waste in the human frame, and Nature gifts
With choicest boons her human worshippers.
How vigorous now the athletic form of age!
How clear its open and unwrinkled brow!
Where neither avarice, cunning, pride, or care,
Had stamped the seal of gray deformity
On all the mingling lineaments of time.
How lovely the intrepid front of youth!
How sweet the smiles of taintless infancy.

Within the massy prison's mouldering courts,
Fearless and free the ruddy children play,
Weaving gay chaplets for their innocent brows
With the green ivy and the red wallflower,
That mock the dungeon's unavailing gloom;
The ponderous chains, and gratings of strong
　　iron,
There rust amid the accumulated ruins

The Dæmon of the World

Now mingling slowly with their native earth:
There the broad beam of day, which feebly
    once
Lighted the cheek of lean captivity
With a pale and sickly glare, now freely shines
On the pure smiles of infant playfulness:
No more the shuddering voice of hoarse despair
Peals through the echoing vaults, but soothing
    notes
Of ivy-fingered winds and gladsome birds
And merriment are resonant around.

   The fanes of Fear and Falsehood hear no
    more
The voice that once waked multitudes to war
Thundering thro' all their aisles: but now re-
    spond
To the death dirge of the melancholy wind:
It were a sight of awfulness to see
The works of faith and slavery, so vast,
So sumptuous, yet withal so perishing!
Even as the corpse that rests beneath their wall.
A thousand mourners deck the pomp of death

The Dæmon of the World

To-day, the breathing marble glows above
To decorate its memory, and tongues
Are busy of its life: to-morrow, worms
In silence and in darkness seize their prey.
These ruins soon leave not a wreck behind:
Their elements, wide-scattered o'er the globe,
To happier shapes are moulded, and become
Ministrant to all blissful impulses:
Thus human things are perfected, and earth,
Even as a child beneath its mother's love,
Is strengthened in all excellence, and grows
Fairer and nobler with each passing year.

Now Time his dusky pennons o'er the scene
Closes in steadfast darkness, and the past
Fades from our charmèd sight. My task is
      done:
Thy lore is learned. Earth's wonders are
      thine own,
With all the fear and all the hope they bring,
My spells are past: the present now recurs.
Ah me! a pathless wilderness remains
Yet unsubdued by man's reclaiming hand.

The Dæmon of the World

Yet, human Spirit, bravely hold thy course,
Let virtue teach thee firmly to pursue
The gradual paths of an aspiring change:
For birth and life and death, and that strange
    state
Before the naked powers that thro' the world
Wander like winds have found a human home,
All tend to perfect happiness, and urge
The restless wheels of being on their way,
Whose flashing spokes, instinct with infinite
    life,
Bicker and burn to gain their destined goal:
For birth but wakes the universal mind
Whose mighty streams might else in silence
    flow
Thro' the vast world, to individual sense
Of outward shows, whose unexperienced shape
New modes of passion to its frame may lend;
Life is its state of action, and the store
Of all events is aggregated there
That variegate the eternal universe;
Death is a gate of dreariness and gloom,
That leads to azure isles and beaming skies

The Dæmon of the World

And happy regions of eternal hope.
Therefore, O Spirit! fearlessly bear on :
Though storms may break the primrose on its
    stalk,
Though frosts may blight the freshness of its
    bloom,
Yet spring's awakening breath will woo the
    earth,
To feed with kindliest dews its favourite
    flower,
That blooms in mossy banks and darksome
    glens,
Lighting the green wood with its sunny smile.

    Fear not then, Spirit, death's disrobing
    hand,
So welcome when the tyrant is awake,
So welcome when the bigot's hell-torch flares ;
'Tis but the voyage of a darksome hour,
The transient gulph-dream of a startling sleep.
For what thou art shall perish utterly,
But what is thine may never cease to be ;
Death is no foe to virtue : earth has seen

The Dæmon of the World

Love's brightest roses on the scaffold bloom,
Mingling with freedom's fadeless laurels there,
And presaging the truth of visioned bliss.
Are there not hopes within thee, which this
    scene
Of linked and gradual being has confirmed?
Hopes that not vainly thou, and living fires
Of mind, as radiant and as pure as thou
Have shone upon the paths of men — return,
Surpassing Spirit, to that world, where thou
Art destined an eternal war to wage
With tyranny and falsehood, and uproot
The germs of misery from the human heart.
Thine is the hand whose piety would soothe
The thorny pillow of unhappy crime,
Whose impotence an easy pardon gains,
Watching its wanderings as a friend's disease:
Thine is the brow whose mildness would defy
Its fiercest rage, and brave its sternest will,
When fenced by power and master of the world.
Thou art sincere and good; of resolute mind,
Free from heart-withering custom's cold con-
    trol,

272

The Dæmon of the World

Of passion lofty, pure and unsubdued.
Earth's pride and meanness could not vanquish
    thee,
And therefore art thou worthy of the boon
Which thou hast now received: virtue shall
    keep
Thy footsteps in the path that thou hast trod,
And many days of beaming hope shall bless
Thy spotless life of sweet and sacred love.
Go, happy one, and give that bosom joy
    Whose sleepless spirit waits to catch
    Light, life and rapture from thy smile.

    The Dæmon called its wingèd ministers
Speechless with bliss the Spirit mounts the car,
That rolled beside the crystal battlement,
Bending her beamy eyes in thankfulness.
    The burning wheels inflame
The steep descent of Heaven's untrodden
    way.
    Fast and far the chariot flew:
    The mighty globes that rolled
Around the gate of the Eternal Fane

The Dæmon of the World

Lessened by slow degrees, and soon appeared
Such tiny twinklers as the planet orbs
That ministering on the solar power
With borrowed light pursued their narrower
    way.
    Earth floated then below:
    The chariot paused a moment;
    The Spirit then descended:
    And from the earth departing
    The shadows with swift wings
Speeded like thought upon the light of
    Heaven.

    The Body and the Soul united then,
A gentle start convulsed Ianthe's frame:
Her veiny eyelids quietly unclosed;
Moveless awhile the dark blue orbs remained:
She looked around in wonder and beheld
Henry, who kneeled in silence by her couch,
Watching her sleep with looks of speechless
    love,
    And the bright beaming stars
    That through the casement shone.

Alastor

Or, The Spirit of Solitude

Preface

———◆———

THE poem entitled "Alastor" may be considered as allegorical of one of the most interesting situations of the human mind. It represents a youth of uncorrupted feelings and adventurous genius led forth by an imagination inflamed and purified through familiarity with all that is excellent and majestic, to the contemplation of the universe. He drinks deep of the fountains of knowledge, and is still insatiate. The magnificence and beauty of the external world sinks profoundly into the frame of his conceptions, and affords to their modifications a variety not to be exhausted. So long as it is possible for his desires to point toward objects thus infinite and unmeasured, he is joyous, and tranquil, and self-possessed. But the period arrives

Preface

when these objects cease to suffice. His mind is at length suddenly awakened and thirsts for intercourse with an intelligence similar to itself. He images to himself the Being whom he loves. Conversant with speculations of the sublimest and most perfect natures, the vision in which he embodies his own imaginations unites all of wonderful, or wise, or beautiful, which the poet, the philosopher, or the lover could depicture. The intellectual faculties, the imagination, the functions of sense, have their respective requisitions on the sympathy of corresponding powers in other human beings. The poet is represented as uniting these requisitions, and attaching them to a single image. He seeks-in vain for a prototype of his conception. Blasted by his disappointment, he descends to an untimely grave.

The picture is not barren of instruction to actual men. The poet's self-centred seclusion was avenged by the furies of an irresistible passion pursuing him to speedy ruin. But that Power which strikes the luminaries of the world with sudden darkness and extinction, by awakening them to too exquisite a perception of its influences, dooms to a slow and poison-

Preface

ous decay those meaner spirits that dare to
abjure its dominion. Their destiny is more
abject and inglorious as their delinquency is
more contemptible and pernicious. They who,
deluded by no generous error, instigated by no
sacred thirst of doubtful knowledge, duped
by no illustrious superstition, loving nothing
on this earth, and cherishing no hopes beyond,
yet keep aloof from sympathies with their
kind, rejoicing neither in human joy nor mourning with human grief; these, and such as they,
have their apportioned curse. They languish,
because none feel with them their common
nature. They are morally dead. They are
neither friends, nor lovers, nor fathers, nor
citizens of the world, nor benefactors of their
country. Among those who attempt to exist
without human sympathy, the pure and tender-
hearted perish through the intensity and passion of their search after its communities, when
the vacancy of their spirit suddenly makes
itself felt. All else, selfish, blind, and torpid,
are those unforeseeing multitudes who consti-
tute, together with their own, the lasting misery
and loneliness of the world. Those who love
not their fellow beings live unfruitful lives,

279

and prepare for their old age a miserable grave.

> " The good die first,
> And those whose hearts are dry as summer dust
> Burn to the socket ! "

December 14, 1815.

Alastor

Or, The Spirit of Solitude

Nondum amabam, et amare amabam, quærebam quid amarem,
amans amare. — *Confess. St. August.*

ARTH, ocean, air, belovèd
brotherhood !
If our great Mother has imbued
my soul
With aught of natural piety to feel
Your love, and recompense the boon with
mine ;
If dewy morn, and odorous noon, and even,
With sunset and its gorgeous ministers,
And solemn midnight's tingling silentness ;
If autumn's hollow sighs in the sere wood,
And winter robing with pure snow and crowns
Of starry ice the gray grass and bare boughs ;

Alastor

If spring's voluptuous pantings, when she
    breathes
Her first sweet kisses, have been dear to me;
If no bright bird, insect, or gentle beast
I consciously have injured, but still loved
And cherished these my kindred; then forgive
This boast, belovèd brethren, and withdraw
No portion of your wonted favour now!

Mother of this unfathomable world!
Favour my solemn song, for I have loved
Thee ever, and thee only: I have watched
Thy shadow, and the darkness of thy steps,
And my heart ever gazes on the depth
Of thy deep mysteries. I have made my bed
In charnels and on coffins, where black death
Keeps record of the trophies won from thee,
Hoping to still these obstinate questionings
Of thee and thine, by forcing some lone ghost,
Thy messenger, to render up the tale
Of what we are. In lone and silent hours,
When night makes a weird sound of its own
    stillness,

Alastor

Like an inspired and desperate alchymist
Staking his very life on some dark hope,
Have I mixed awful talk and asking looks
With my most innocent love, until strange
    tears,
Uniting with those breathless kisses, made
Such magic as compels the charmèd night
To render up thy charge: . . . and, though
    ne'er yet
Thou hast unveiled thy inmost sanctuary,
Enough from incommunicable dream,
And twilight phantasms, and deep noonday
    thought,
Has shone within me, that serenely now
And moveless, as a long-forgotten lyre
Suspended in the solitary dome
Of some mysterious and deserted fane,
I wait thy breath, Great Parent, that my
    strain
May modulate with murmurs of the air,
And motions of the forests and the sea,
And voice of living beings, and woven hymns
Of night and day, and the deep heart of man.

Alastor

There was a Poet whose untimely tomb
No human hands with pious reverence reared,
But the charmed eddies of autumnal winds
Built o'er his mouldering bones a pyramid
Of mouldering leaves in the waste wilder-
    ness : —
A lovely youth, — no mourning maiden decked
With weeping flowers, or votive cypress
    wreath,
The lone couch of his everlasting sleep : —
Gentle, and brave, and generous, — no lorn
    bard
Breathed o'er his dark fate one melodious
    sigh :
He lived, he died, he sung, in solitude.
Strangers have wept to hear his passionate
    notes,
And virgins, as unknown he passed, have
    pined
And wasted for fond love of his wild eyes.
The fire of those soft orbs has ceased to burn,
And Silence, too enamoured of that voice,
Locks its mute music in her rugged cell.

Alastor

By solemn vision, and bright silver dream,
His infancy was nurtured.   Every sight
And sound from the vast earth and ambient
    air
Sent to his heart its choicest impulses.
The fountains of divine philosophy
Fled not his thirsting lips, and all of great,
Or good, or lovely, which the sacred past
In truth or fable consecrates, he felt
And knew. When early youth had passed, he
    left
His cold fireside and alienated home
To seek strange truths in undiscovered lands.
Many a wide waste and tangled wilderness
Has lured his fearless steps ; and he has bought
With his sweet voice and eyes, from savage
    men,
His rest and food. Nature's most secret steps
He like her shadow has pursued, where'er
The red volcano overcanopies
Its fields of snow and pinnacles of ice
With burning smoke, or where bitumen lakes
On black bare pointed islets ever beat

Alastor

With sluggish surge, or where the secret caves
Rugged and dark, winding among the springs
Of fire and poison, inaccessible
To avarice or pride, their starry domes
Of diamond and of gold expand above
Numberless and immeasurable halls,
Frequent with crystal column, and clear shrines
Of pearl, and thrones radiant with chrysolite.
Nor had that scene of ampler majesty
Than gems or gold, the varying roof of heaven
And the green earth, lost in his heart its claims
To love and wonder; he would linger long
In lonesome vales, making the wild his home,
Until the doves and squirrels would partake
From his innocuous hand his bloodless food,
Lured by the gentle meaning of his looks,
And the wild antelope, that starts whene'er
The dry leaf rustles in the brake, suspend
Her timid steps to gaze upon a form
More graceful than her own.
                              His wandering step,
Obedient to high thoughts, has visited
The awful ruins of the days of old:

Alastor

Athens, and Tyre, and Balbec, and the waste
Where stood Jerusalem, the fallen towers
Of Babylon, the eternal pyramids,
Memphis and Thebes, and whatsoe'er of
    strange
Sculptured on alabaster obelisk,
Or jasper tomb, or mutilated sphinx,
Dark Æthiopia in her desert hills
Conceals.   Among the ruined temples there,
Stupendous columns, and wild images
Of more than man, where marble dæmons
    watch
The Zodiac's brazen mystery, and dead men
Hang their mute thoughts on the mute walls
    around,
He lingered, poring on memorials
Of the world's youth, through the long burn-
    ing day
Gazed on those speechless shapes, nor, when
    the moon
Filled the mysterious halls with floating shades,
Suspended he that task, but ever gazed
And gazed, till meaning on his vacant mind

Alastor

Flashed like strong inspiration, and he saw
The thrilling secrets of the birth of time.

   Meanwhile an Arab maiden brought his
     food,
Her daily portion, from her father's tent,
And spread her matting for his couch, and
     stole
From duties and repose to tend his steps : —
Enamoured, yet not daring for deep awe
To speak her love : — and watched his nightly
     sleep,
Sleepless herself, to gaze upon his lips
Parted in slumber, whence the regular breath
Of innocent dreams arose : then, when red
     morn
Made paler the pale moon, to her cold home,
Wildered, and wan, and panting, she returned.

   The Poet, wandering on, through Arabie
And Persia, and the wild Carmanian waste,
And o'er the aërial mountains which pour
     down

Alastor

Indus and Oxus from their icy caves,
In joy and exultation held his way;
Till in the vale of Cashmire, far within
Its loneliest dell, where odorous plants entwine
Beneath the hollow rocks a natural bower,
Beside a sparkling rivulet he stretched
His languid limbs.   A vision on his sleep
There came, a dream of hopes that never yet
Had flushed his cheek.   He dreamed a veilèd
      maid
Sate near him, talking in low solemn tones.
Her voice was like the voice of his own soul
Heard in the calm of thought; its music long,
Like woven sounds of streams and breezes,
      held
His inmost sense suspended in its web
Of many-coloured woof and shifting hues.
Knowledge   and   truth   and   virtue   were   her
      theme,
And lofty hopes of divine liberty,
Thoughts the most dear to him, and poesy,
Herself a poet.   Soon the solemn mood
Of her pure mind kindled through all her frame

Alastor

A permeating fire: wild numbers then
She raised, with voice stifled in tremulous sobs
Subdued by its own pathos: her fair hands
Were bare alone, sweeping from some strange
    harp
Strange symphony, and in their branching veins
The eloquent blood told an ineffable tale.
The beating of her heart was heard to fill
The pauses of her music, and her breath
Tumultuously accorded with those fits
Of intermitted song. Sudden she rose,
As if her heart impatiently endured
Its bursting burthen: at the sound he turned,
And saw by the warm light of their own life
Her glowing limbs beneath the sinuous veil
Of woven wind, her outspread arms now bare,
Her dark locks floating in the breath of night,
Her beamy bending eyes, her parted lips
Outstretched and pale, and quivering eagerly.
His strong heart sunk and sickened with excess
Of love. He reared his shuddering limbs and
    quelled
His gasping breath, and spread his arms to meet

Alastor

Her panting bosom : . . . she drew back a
    while,
Then, yielding to the irresistible joy,
With frantic gesture and short breathless cry
Folded his frame in her dissolving arms.
Now blackness veiled his dizzy eyes, and
    night
Involved and swallowed up the vision; sleep,
Like a dark flood suspended in its course,
Rolled back its impulse on his vacant brain.

Roused by the shock he started from his
    trance —
The cold white light of morning, the blue
    moon
Low in the west, the clear and garish hills,
The distinct valley and the vacant woods,
Spread round him where he stood.   Whither
    have fled
The hues of heaven that canopied his bower
Of yesternight ?   The sounds that soothed his
    sleep,
The mystery and the majesty of Earth,

Alastor

The joy, the exultation ?   His wan eyes
Gaze on the empty scene as vacantly
As ocean's moon looks on the moon in
   heaven.
The spirit of sweet human love has sent
A vision to the sleep of him who spurned
Her choicest gifts.   He eagerly pursues
Beyond the realms of dream that fleeting
   shade ;
He overleaps the bounds.   Alas ! alas !
Were limbs, and breath, and being intertwined
Thus treacherously ?   Lost, lost, for ever lost,
In the wide pathless desert of dim sleep,
That beautiful shape !   Does the dark gate of
   death
Conduct to thy mysterious paradise,
O Sleep ?   Does the bright arch of rainbow
   clouds,
And pendent mountains seen in the calm
   lake,
Lead only to a black and watery depth,
While death's blue vault, with loathliest va-
   pours hung,

Alastor

Where every shade which the foul grave ex-
    hales
Hides its dead eye from the detested day,
Conduct, O Sleep, to thy delightful realms?
This doubt with sudden tide flowed on his
    heart;
The insatiate hope which it awakened stung
His brain even like despair.
                While daylight held
The sky, the Poet kept mute conference
With his still soul. At night the passion
    came,
Like the fierce fiend of a distempered dream,
And shook him from his rest, and led him
    forth
Into the darkness. — As an eagle, grasped
In folds of the green serpent, feels her breast
Burn with the poison, and precipitates
Through night and day, tempest, and calm,
    and cloud,
Frantic with dizzying anguish, her blind flight
O'er the wide aery wilderness: thus driven
By the bright shadow of that lovely dream,

Alastor

Beneath the cold glare of the desolate night,
Through tangled swamps and deep precipitous
    dells,
Startling with careless step the moonlight
    snake,
He fled. Red morning dawned upon his
    flight,
Shedding the mockery of its vital hues
Upon his cheek of death. He wandered on
Till vast Aornos seen from Petra's steep
Hung o'er the low horizon like a cloud;
Through Balk, and where the desolated tombs
Of Parthian kings scatter to every wind
Their wasting dust, wildly he wandered on,
Day after day, a weary waste of hours,
Bearing within his life the brooding care
That ever fed on its decaying flame.
And now his limbs were lean; his scattered
    hair
Sered by the autumn of strange suffering
Sung dirges in the wind; his listless hand
Hung like dead bone within its withered skin;
Life, and the lustre that consumed it, shone

Alastor

As in a furnace burning secretly
From his dark eyes alone.   The cottagers,
Who ministered with human charity
His human wants, beheld with wondering awe
Their fleeting visitant.   The mountaineer,
Encountering on some dizzy precipice
That spectral form, deemed that the Spirit of
    wind
With lightning eyes, and eager breath, and feet
Disturbing not the drifted snow, had paused
In its career: the infant would conceal
His troubled visage in his mother's robe
In terror at the glare of those wild eyes,
To remember their strange light in many a
    dream
Of after-times; but youthful maidens, taught
By nature, would interpret half the woe
That wasted him, would call him with false
    names
Brother, and friend, would press his pallid hand
At parting, and watch, dim through tears, the
    path
Of his departure from their father's door.

Alastor

At length upon the lone Chorasmian shore
He paused, a wide and melancholy waste
Of putrid marshes.   A strong impulse urged
His steps to the seashore.   A swan was there,
Beside a sluggish stream among the reeds.
It rose as he approached, and with strong
    wings
Scaling the upward sky, bent its bright course
High over the immeasurable main.
His eyes pursued its flight. — "Thou hast a
    home,
Beautiful bird; thou voyagest to thine home,
Where thy sweet mate will twine her downy
    neck
With thine, and welcome thy return with eyes
Bright in the lustre of their own fond joy.
And what am I that I should linger here,
With voice far sweeter than thy dying notes,
Spirit more vast than thine, frame more attuned
To beauty, wasting these surpassing powers
In the deaf air, to the blind earth, and heaven
That echoes not my thoughts?"   A gloomy
    smile

Alastor

Of desperate hope wrinkled his quivering
lips.
For sleep, he knew, kept most relentlessly
Its precious charge, and silent death exposed,
Faithless perhaps as sleep, a shadowy lure,
With doubtful smile mocking its own strange
charms.

Startled by his own thoughts he looked
around.
There was no fair fiend near him, not a sight
Or sound of awe but in his own deep mind.
A little shallop floating near the shore
Caught the impatient wandering of his gaze.
It had been long abandoned, for its sides
Gaped wide with many a rift, and its frail
joints
Swayed with the undulations of the tide.
A restless impulse urged him to embark
And meet lone Death on the drear ocean's
waste ;
For well he knew that mighty Shadow loves
The slimy caverns of the populous deep.

Alastor

The day was fair and sunny, sea and sky
Drank its inspiring radiance, and the wind
Swept strongly from the shore, blackening the
    waves.
Following his eager soul, the wanderer
Leaped in the boat, he spread his cloak aloft
On the bare mast, and took his lonely seat,
And felt the boat speed o'er the tranquil sea
Like a torn cloud before the hurricane.

As one that in a silver vision floats
Obedient to the sweep of odorous winds
Upon resplendent clouds, so rapidly
Along the dark and ruffled waters fled
The straining boat. — A whirlwind swept it on,
With fierce gusts and precipitating force,
Through the white ridges of the chafèd sea.
The waves arose.   Higher and higher still
Their fierce necks writhed beneath the tempest's
    scourge
Like serpents struggling in a vulture's grasp.
Calm and rejoicing in the fearful war
Of wave ruining on wave, and blast on blast

Alastor

Descending, and black flood on whirlpool
  driven
With dark obliterating course, he sate:
As if their genii were the ministers
Appointed to conduct him to the light
Of those belovèd eyes, the Poet sate
Holding the steady helm.   Evening came on,
The beams of sunset hung their rainbow hues
High 'mid the shifting domes of sheeted spray
That canopied his path o'er the waste deep;
Twilight, ascending slowly from the east,
Entwined in duskier wreaths her braided locks
O'er the fair front and radiant eyes of day;
Night followed, clad with stars.   On every side
More horribly the multitudinous streams
Of ocean's mountainous waste to mutual war
Rushed in dark tumult thundering, as to mock
The calm and spangled sky.   The little boat
Still fled before the storm; still fled, like foam
Down the steep cataract of a wintry river;
Now pausing on the edge of the riven wave;
Now leaving far behind the bursting mass
That fell, convulsing ocean.   Safely fled —

Alastor

As if that frail and wasted human form,
Had been an elemental god.
                    At midnight
The moon arose : and lo ! the ethereal cliffs
Of Caucasus, whose icy summits shone
Among the stars like sunlight, and around
Whose caverned base the whirlpools and the
    waves
Bursting and eddying irresistibly
Rage and resound for ever. — Who shall
    save ? —
The boat fled on, — the boiling torrent drove,—
The crags closed round with black and jaggèd
    arms,
The shattered mountain overhung the sea,
And faster still, beyond all human speed,
Suspended on the sweep of the smooth wave,
The little boat was driven.   A cavern there
Yawned, and amid its slant and winding
    depths
Ingulphed the rushing sea.   The boat fled on
With unrelaxing speed. — "Vision and Love !"
The Poet cried aloud, " I have beheld

Alastor

The path of thy departure.   Sleep and death
Shall not divide us long!"

                        The boat pursued
The windings of the cavern.   Daylight shone
At length upon that gloomy river's flow;
Now, where the fiercest war among the waves
Is calm, on the unfathomable stream
The boat moved slowly.   Where the moun-
      tain, riven,
Exposed those black depths to the azure sky,
Ere yet the flood's enormous volume fell
Even to the base of Caucasus, with sound
That shook the everlasting rocks, the mass
Filled with one whirlpool all that ample chasm:
Stair above stair the eddying waters rose,
Circling immeasurably fast, and laved
With alternating dash the gnarlèd roots
Of mighty trees, that stretched their giant arms
In darkness over it.   I' the midst was left,
Reflecting, yet distorting every cloud,
A pool of treacherous and tremendous calm.
Seized by the sway of the ascending stream,

Alastor

With dizzy swiftness, round, and round, and
    round,
Ridge after ridge the straining boat arose,
Till on the verge of the extremest curve,
Where, through an opening of the rocky bank,
The waters overflow, and a smooth spot
Of glassy quiet mid those battling tides
Is left, the boat paused shuddering. — Shall it
    sink
Down the abyss? Shall the reverting stress
Of that resistless gulph embosom it?
Now shall it fall? — A wandering stream of
    wind,
Breathed from the west, has caught the ex-
    panded sail,
And, lo! with gentle motion, between banks
Of mossy slope, and on a placid stream,
Beneath a woven grove it sails, and, hark!
The ghastly torrent mingles its far roar,
With the breeze murmuring in the musical
    woods.
Where the embowering trees recede, and leave
A little space of green expanse, the cove

Alastor

Is closed by meeting banks, whose yellow
  flowers
For ever gaze on their own drooping eyes,
Reflected in the crystal calm.   The wave
Of the boat's motion marred their pensive task,
Which nought but vagrant bird, or wanton
  wind,
Or falling spear-grass, or their own decay
Had e'er disturbed before.   The Poet longed
To deck with their bright hues his withered
  hair,
But on his heart its solitude returned,
And he forebore.   Not the strong impulse
  hid
In those flushed cheeks, bent eyes, and
  shadowy frame
Had yet performed its ministry : it hung
Upon his life, as lightning in a cloud
Gleams, hovering ere it vanish, ere the floods
Of night close over it.
                    The noonday sun
Now shone upon the forest, one vast mass
Of mingling shade, whose brown magnificence

Alastor

A narrow vale embosoms.   There, huge caves,
Scooped in the dark base of their aery rocks
Mocking its moans, respond and roar for ever.
The meeting boughs and implicated leaves
Wove twilight o'er the Poet's path, as led
By love, or dream, or god, or mightier Death,
He sought in Nature's dearest haunt, some
    bank,
Her cradle, and his sepulchre.   More dark
And dark the shades accumulate.   The oak,
Expanding its immense and knotty arms,
Embraces the light beech.   The pyramids
Of the tall cedar overarching frame
Most solemn domes within, and far below,
Like clouds suspended in an emerald sky,
The ash and the acacia floating hang
Tremulous and pale.   Like restless serpents,
    clothed
In rainbow and in fire, the parasites,
Starred with ten thousand blossoms, flow
    around
The gray trunks, and, as gamesome infants'
    eyes,

Alastor

With gentle meanings, and most innocent
    wiles,
Fold their beams round the hearts of those
    that love,
These twine their tendrils with the wedded
    boughs
Uniting their close union; the woven leaves
Make net-work of the dark blue light of day,
And the night's noontide clearness, mutable
As shapes in the weird clouds.   Soft mossy
    lawns
Beneath these canopies extend their swells,
Fragrant with perfumed herbs, and eyed with
    blooms
Minute yet beautiful.   One darkest glen
Sends from its woods of musk-rose, twined
    with jasmine,
A soul-dissolving odour, to invite
To some more lovely mystery.   Through the
    dell,
Silence and Twilight here, twin-sisters, keep
Their noonday watch, and sail among the
    shades,

Alastor

Like vapourous shapes half-seen; beyond, a
    well,
Dark, gleaming, and of most translucent wave,
Images all the woven boughs above,
And each depending leaf, and every speck
Of azure sky, darting between their chasms
Nor aught else in the liquid mirror laves
Its portraiture, but some inconstant star
Between one foliaged lattice twinkling fair,
Or painted bird, sleeping beneath the moon,
Or gorgeous insect floating motionless,
Unconscious of the day, ere yet his wings
Have spread their glories to the gaze of noon.

Hither the Poet came.   His eyes beheld
Their own wan light through the reflected lines
Of his thin hair, distinct in the dark depth
Of that still fountain; as the human heart,
Gazing in dreams over the gloomy grave,
Sees its own treacherous likeness there.   He
    heard
The motion of the leaves, the grass that sprung
Startled and glanced and trembled even to feel

Alastor

An unaccustomed presence, and the sound
Of the sweet brook that from the secret springs
Of that dark fountain rose.   A Spirit seemed
To stand beside him — clothed in no bright
      robes
Of shadowy silver or enshrining light,
Borrowed from aught the visible world affords
Of grace, or majesty, or mystery ; —
But undulating woods, and silent well,
And leaping rivulet, and evening gloom
Now deepening the dark shades, for speech
      assuming,
Held commune with him, as if he and it
Were all that was, — only . . . when his re-
      gard
Was raised by intense pensiveness, . . . two
      eyes,
Two starry eyes, hung in the gloom of thought,
And seemed with their serene and azure smiles
To beckon him.

            Obedient to the light
That shone within his soul, he went, pursuing

Alastor

The windings of the dell. — The rivulet
Wanton and wild, through many a green
    ravine
Beneath the forest flowed. Sometimes it fell
Among the moss with hollow harmony
Dark and profound. Now on the polished
    stones
It danced; like childhood laughing as it went:
Then through the plain in tranquil wanderings
    crept,
Reflecting every herb and drooping bud
That overhung its quietness. — " O stream!
Whose source is inaccessibly profound,
Whither do thy mysterious waters tend?
Thou imagest my life. Thy darksome still-
    ness,
Thy dazzling waves, thy loud and hollow
    gulphs,
Thy searchless fountain, and invisible course
Have each their type in me: and the wide
    sky,
And measureless ocean may declare as soon
What oozy cavern or what wandering cloud

Alastor

Contains thy waters, as the universe
Tell where these living thoughts reside, when
    stretched
Upon thy flowers my bloodless limbs shall
    waste
I' the passing wind!"

                    Beside the grassy shore
Of the small stream he went; he did impress
On the green moss his tremulous step, that
    caught
Strong shuddering from his burning limbs.
    As one
Roused by some joyous madness from the
    couch
Of fever, he did move, yet not like him
Forgetful of the grave, where, when the flame
Of his frail exultation shall be spent,
He must descend. With rapid steps he went
Beneath the shade of trees, beside the flow
Of the wild babbling rivulet; and now
The forest's solemn canopies were changed
For the uniform and lightsome evening sky.

Alastor

Gray rocks did peep from the spare moss, and
  stemmed
The struggling brook : tall spires of windlestrae
Threw their thin shadows down the rugged
  slope,
And nought but gnarled roots of ancient pines,
Branchless and blasted, clenched with grasping
  roots
The unwilling soil.   A gradual change was
  here,
Yet ghastly.   For, as fast years flow away,
The smooth brow gathers, and the hair grows
  thin
And white, and where irradiate dewy eyes
Had shone, gleam stony orbs : — so from his
  steps
Bright flowers departed, and the beautiful shade
Of the green groves, with all their odorous
  winds
And musical motions. Calm, he still pursued
The stream, that with a larger volume now
Rolled through the labyrinthine dell, and there
Fretted a path through its descending curves

Alastor

With its wintry speed. On every side now
    rose
Rocks, which, in unimaginable forms,
Lifted their black and barren pinnacles
In the light of evening, and, its precipice
Obscuring the ravine, disclosed above,
Mid toppling stones, black gulphs and yawn-
    ing caves,
Whose windings gave ten thousand various
    tongues
To the loud stream. Lo! where the pass
    expands
Its stony jaws, the abrupt mountain breaks,
And seems, with its accumulated crags,
To overhang the world: for wide expand
Beneath the wan stars and descending moon
Islanded seas, blue mountains, mighty streams,
Dim tracts and vast, robed in the lustrous
    gloom
Of leaden-coloured even, and fiery hills
Mingling their flames with twilight, on the
    verge
Of the remote horizon. The near scene,

Alastor

In naked and severe simplicity,
Made contrast with the universe. A pine,
Rock-rooted, stretched athwart the vacancy
Its swinging boughs, to each inconstant blast
Yielding one only response, at each pause
In most familiar cadence, with the howl,
The thunder and the hiss of homeless streams
Mingling its solemn song, whilst the broad
    river,
Foaming and hurrying o'er its rugged path,
Fell into that immeasurable void
Scattering its waters to the passing winds.

  Yet the gray precipice and solemn pine
And torrent were not all; — one silent nook
Was there. Even on the edge of that vast
    mountain,
Upheld by knotty roots and fallen rocks,
It overlooked in its serenity
The dark earth, and the bending vault of stars.
It was a tranquil spot, that seemed to smile
Even in the lap of horror. Ivy clasped
The fissured stones with its entwining arms,

Alastor

And did embower with leaves for ever green,
And berries dark, the smooth and even space
Of its inviolated floor, and here
The children of the autumnal whirlwind bore,
In wanton sport, those bright leaves, whose
  decay,
Red, yellow, or ethereally pale,
Rivals the pride of summer.   'Tis the haunt
Of every gentle wind, whose breath can
  teach
The wilds to love tranquillity.   One step,
One human step alone, has ever broken
The stillness of its solitude : — one voice
Alone inspired its echoes ; — even that voice
Which hither came, floating among the winds,
And led the loveliest among human forms
To make their wild haunts the depository
Of all the grace and beauty that endued
Its motions, render up its majesty,
Scatter its music on the unfeeling storm,
And to the damp leaves and blue cavern
  mould,
Nurses of rainbow flowers and branching moss,

Alastor

Commit the colours of that varying cheek,
That snowy breast, those dark and drooping
    eyes.

    The dim and hornèd moon hung low, and
    poured
A sea of lustre on the horizon's verge
That overflowed its mountains.   Yellow mist
Filled the unbounded atmosphere, and drank
Wan moonlight even to fulness: not a star
Shone, not a sound was heard; the very winds,
Danger's grim playmates, on that precipice
Slept, clasped in his embrace. — O, storm of
    death !
Whose sightless speed divides this sullen
    night:
And thou, colossal Skeleton, that, still
Guiding its irresistible career
In thy devastating omnipotence,
Art king of this frail world, from the red field
Of slaughter, from the reeking hospital,
The patriot's sacred couch, the snowy bed
Of innocence, the scaffold and the throne,

Alastor

A mighty voice invokes thee.   Ruin calls
His brother Death.   A rare and regal prey
He hath prepared, prowling around the world;
Glutted with which thou mayst repose, and
    men
Go to their graves like flowers or creeping
    worms,
Nor ever more offer at thy dark shrine
The unheeded tribute of a broken heart.

   When on the threshold of the green recess
The wanderer's footsteps fell, he knew that
    death
Was on him.   Yet a little, ere it fled,
Did he resign his high and holy soul
To images of the majestic past,
That paused within his passive being now,
Like winds that bear sweet music, when they
    breathe
Through some dim latticed chamber.   He
    did place
His pale lean hand upon the rugged trunk
Of the old pine.   Upon an ivied stone

Alastor

Reclined his languid head, his limbs did rest,
Diffused and motionless, on the smooth brink
Of that obscurest chasm ; — and thus he lay,
Surrendering to their final impulses
The hovering powers of life. Hope and
    despair,
The torturers, slept ; no mortal pain or fear
Marred his repose, the influxes of sense,
And his own being unalloyed by pain,
Yet feebler and more feeble, calmly fed
The stream of thought, till he lay breathing
    there
At peace, and faintly smiling : — his last sight
Was the great moon, which o'er the western
    line
Of the wide world her mighty horn suspended,
With whose dun beams inwoven darkness
    seemed
To mingle. Now upon the jaggèd hills
It rests, and still as the divided frame
Of the vast meteor sunk, the Poet's blood,
That ever beat in mystic sympathy
With nature's ebb and flow, grew feebler still :

Alastor

And when two lessening points of light alone
Gleamed through the darkness, the alternate
    gasp
Of his faint respiration scarce did stir
The stagnate night : — till the minutest ray
Was quenched, the pulse yet lingered in his
    heart.
It paused — it fluttered. But when heaven
    remained
Utterly black, the murky shades involved
An image, silent, cold, and motionless
As their own voiceless earth and vacant air.
Even as a vapour fed with golden beams
That ministered on sunlight, ere the west
Eclipses it, was now that wondrous frame —
No sense, no motion, no divinity —
A fragile lute, on whose harmonious strings
The breath of heaven did wander — a bright
    stream
Once fed with many-voicèd waves — a dream
Of youth, which night and time have quenched
    for ever,
Still, dark, and dry, and unremembered now.

Alastor

O, for Medea's wondrous alchemy,
Which wheresoe'er it fell made the earth
  gleam
With bright flowers, and the wintry boughs
  exhale
From vernal blooms fresh fragrance! O, that
  God,
Profuse of poisons, would concede the chalice
Which but one living man has drained, who
  now,
Vessel of deathless wrath, a slave that feels
No proud exemption in the blighting curse
He bears, over the world wanders for ever,
Lone as incarnate death! O, that the dream
Of dark magician in his visioned cave,
Raking the cinders of a crucible
For life and power, even when his feeble hand
Shakes in its last decay, were the true law
Of this so lovely world! But thou art fled
Like some frail exhalation; which the dawn
Robes in its golden beams, — ah! thou hast
  fled!
The brave, the gentle, and the beautiful,

318

Alastor

The child of grace and genius.   Heartless
    things
Are done and said i' the world, and many
    worms
And beasts and men live on, and mighty
    Earth
From sea and mountain, city and wilderness,
In vesper low or joyous orison,
Lifts still its solemn voice! — but thou art
    fled —
Thou canst no longer know or love the shapes
Of this phantasmal scene, who have to thee
Been purest ministers, who are, alas!
Now thou art not.   Upon those pallid lips
So sweet even in their silence, on those eyes
That image sleep in death, upon that form
Yet safe from the worm's outrage, let no tear
Be shed — not even in thought.   Nor, when
    those hues
Are gone, and those divinest lineaments,
Worn by the senseless wind, shall live alone
In the frail pauses of this simple strain,
Let not high verse, mourning the memory

Of that which is no more, or painting's woe,
Or sculpture speak in feeble imagery
Their own cold powers.   Art and eloquence,
And all the shows o' the world, are frail and
    vain
To weep a loss that turns their lights to shade.
It is a woe too " deep for tears " when all
Is reft at once, when some surpassing Spirit,
Whose light adorned the world around it,
    leaves
Those who remain behind, not sobs or groans,
The passionate tumult of a clinging hope;
But pale despair and cold tranquillity,
Nature's vast frame, the web of human things,
Birth and the grave, that are not as they were.

Note on Alastor, by Mrs. Shelley

"ALASTOR" is written in a very different tone from "Queen Mab." In the latter, Shelley poured out all the cherished speculations of his youth — all the irrepressible emotions of sympathy, censure, and hope, to which the present suffering, and what he considers the proper destiny, of his fellow creatures, gave birth. "Alastor," on the contrary, contains an individual interest only. A very few years, with their attendant events, had checked the ardour of Shelley's hopes, though he still thought them well grounded, and that to advance their fulfilment was the noblest task man could achieve.

Note on Alastor

This is neither the time nor place to speak
of the misfortunes that chequered his life. It
will be sufficient to say that, in all he did, he
at the time of doing it believed himself justified to his own conscience; while the various
ills of poverty and loss of friends brought
home to him the sad realities of life. Physical
suffering had also considerable influence in
causing him to turn his eyes inward; inclin-
ing him rather to brood over the thoughts
and emotions of his own soul than to glance
abroad, and to make, as in " Queen Mab,"
the whole universe the object and subject
of his song. In the spring of 1815 an eminent physician pronounced that he was dying
rapidly of a consumption; abscesses were
formed on his lungs, and he suffered acute
spasms. Suddenly a complete change took
place; and, though through life he was a
martyr to pain and debility, every symptom
of pulmonary disease vanished. His nerves,
which nature had formed sensitive to an unexampled degree, were rendered still more susceptible by the state of his health.

As soon as the peace of 1814 had opened
the Continent, he went abroad. He visited

Note on Alastor

some of the more magnificent scenes of Switzerland, and returned to England from Lucerne
by the Reuss and the Rhine. The river navi-
gation enchanted him. In his favourite poem
of "Thalaba," his imagination had been excited
by a description of such a voyage. In the
summer of 1815, after a tour along the southern coast of Devonshire and a visit to Clifton,
he rented a house on Bishopgate Heath, on
the borders of Windsor Forest, where he enjoyed several months of comparative health
and tranquil happiness. The later summer
months were warm and dry. Accompanied
by a few friends, he visited the source of the
Thames, making a voyage in a wherry from
Windsor to Cricklade. His beautiful stanzas
in the churchyard of Lechlade were written on
that occasion. "Alastor" was composed on
his return. He spent his days under the oak-
shades of Windsor Great Park; and the magnificent woodland was a fitting study to inspire
the various descriptions of forest scenery we
find in the poem.

None of Shelley's poems is more characteristic than this. The solemn spirit that reigns
throughout, the worship of the majesty of

nature, the broodings of a poet's heart in solitude, — the mingling of the exulting joy which the various aspects of the visible universe inspires with the sad and struggling pangs which human passion imparts, — give a touching interest to the whole. The death which he had often contemplated during the last months as certain and near he here represented in such colours as had, in his lonely musings, soothed his soul to peace. The versification sustains the solemn spirit which breathes throughout: it is peculiarly melodious. The poem ought rather to be considered didactic than narrative: it was the outpouring of his own emotions, embodied in the purest form he could conceive, painted in the ideal hues which his brilliant imagination inspired, and softened by the recent anticipation of death.

THE END.

CPSIA information can be obtained
at www.ICGtesting.com
Printed in the USA
BVHW051217241221
624765BV00003B/142